BEAUTY Before BRITTANY

A SELF~DISCOVERY JOURNEY & BIBLE STUDY

DANA McCARTNEY CANDILLO, BSN, RN

Purpose Publishing
1503 Main Street #168 ⁕ Grandview, Missouri
www.purposepublishing.com

Copyright © 2016 Dana McCartney Candillo

ISBN: 978-0-9861063-8-5

Editing by Rae Lewis & Esile Potter
Book Cover Design by Thaddeus Jordan

No part of this publication may be reproduced, stored in retrieval system, or transmitted in any form or by any means, electronic, mechanical, photo copying, recording, scanning, or otherwise, except as permitted under Section 107 or 108 of the United States Copyright Act, without either the prior written permission of the Publisher.

This journey and discovery workbook was created to allow for the reader to choose of her own free will to participate in her own journaling and study methods. This guide along with published literature is presented as a helpful resource for self-help and wellness. The author/ publisher are not advisors or counselors yet are ministers, prayer partners and lay people praying for your highest outcome while on the journey.

All scripture contained in this book are referenced from the New King James Version, The Message, New Living Translation, Amplified and New International Versions of the Bible.

Printed in the United States of America.

A Special Dedication

To My Daughters & Nieces,
May you always look to God's Word to seek answers, find solutions, and apply Truth to every life circumstance and daily living. I pray that you will have continued wisdom, knowledge, and revelation of who HE IS and who YOU ARE as you search the Bible, the Living Word where all accurate and infallible teaching and instruction exist. It is the source of our true identity and the Well of Life!
~Mom

To All Pastor's Wives,
If there is one thing that I have honored and held dear, it is the Favor and Incredible support of so many Pastors' wives! You have made my ability to become vulnerable and transparent in ministry more courageous, brave, and fearless! For this I am forever grateful. Without the love, acceptance, and push of Godly Women, Mentors, and Examples, I would not have been able to break the chains of fear of judgmental spirits inside the church walls with integrity and credibility. Knowing that the most important thing is to please God and not man! With True Freedom of Expression and Power in Testimony, souls are won to Christ and the Great Commission is Accomplished! Thank You!
&
To all Women's Ministry Leaders,
I pray that this Self-Discovery Journey & Bible Study will be a tool that will be so effective and instrumental in guiding women into His Grace, Mercy, Forgiveness, Image, and Revelation of a Magnificent, Transformational Relationship with Jesus!

~Dana

Praise for BBB

Dana says…"Often times we are **one decision** away from creating change and shifting the direction of our entire lives." I believe in what Dana is saying on these pages and I look forward to the healing it will bring to many women as she passes the baton of a redemption story. **Rosemarie Clair, Lead Pastor's Wife/Women's Ministry Leader at Tiffany Fellowship Church, Kansas City, MO**

Beauty Before Brittany is not your typical self-help book. Dana takes the reader on a journey and helps her discover her destiny by giving practical ways to unlock her pain, passion and purpose. This book will certainly be a treasure to any woman on the road to hope and wholeness. **Annette Westlake, First Lady, Sheffield Family Life Center, Kansas City, MO**

"Dana has a genuine ability to display God's love to women caught in the sex trafficking industry. Her ideas inside this book are sure to help women coming out of this lifestyle begin to see the difference between the way God sees them and the way the world has taught them to see themselves. -" **Clint Thomas, MA, LPC**

Many themes run through this study and story. One is the powerful role that Dana's unconditional love and affection plays in loving what others may see as the unlovable. I stand in awe of Dana's boldness, determination, and courage to assist and love the women caught in this industry. God's call on her life is real and she has the courage to fulfill the vision He has given her! **Dr. Vickie Murillo, Wife of Pastor Willie Murillo of Sheffield Family Life Center, Kansas City, MO Mother of Two and an Urban Educator**

Whether this book is used outside the walls of the church or in women's ministries, it is a vibrant & remarkable resource of self-discovery and soul searching study of the Word that is engaging and far reaching for any woman and is absolutely multi-generational. Perfect for any woman seeking change, hope, & growth! **Lisa Purkey, Co-Pastor, Nexus Church, Lenexa, Kansas**

Dana is a beautiful example of a woman lost who was transformed by the loving gentle arms of Christ into a magnificent butterfly. Her story guides the reader through her personal abuse, tragedy and loss to an awakening of truth, hope and love and ultimately her life's redemptive purpose. She then directs readers how to navigate their personal painful losses toward unlocking the keys to their passion and purposes in Christ. *Beauty Before Brittany* will challenge, motivate and activate its' readers to live out their God given destinies from heaven.

Annie Lobert, Founder & President Hookers For Jesus and Destiny House (safe house for sex trafficked women), Author of book *Fallen: Out of the Sex Industry & Into the Arms of the Savior*, Las Vegas, NV

Note to Reader:

It is suggested to get maximum benefit of this study guide and journal is to first read, **Surrendered Showgirl** by Dana McCartney Candillo. By reading her book first, you will gain an inside perspective of how her life was powerfully transformed by the power of God! It's not just her story, but her personal testimony. Dana shares the intimate details of her life and what changes she was able to make to give her a new and beautiful life. You too can experience your own transformation within the pages of this book and study guide.

Table of Contents

Introduction……………………………………………………9
A Word from the Author………………………………………13

Section 1: UNLOCKING YOUR PAIN
Chapter One
      Uncover………………………………………………...19
Chapter Two
      Wretched Rags to Royal Riches……………………...23

Section 2: UNLOCKING YOUR PASSION
Chapter Three
      Gazing into God's Mirror…………………...…….......43
Chapter Four
      Finding Hope in God……………………………..……71

Section 3: UNLOCKING YOUR PURPOSE
Chapter Five
      Discovering Your True Reflection………………...…97
Chapter Six
      Seeing Me the Way God Sees Me………………...…115

Section 4: OPEN THE DOOR TO YOUR DESTINY
Chapter Seven
      Daughter of the King……………………………..........121
Chapter Eight
      It's Time………..…………………………………....…127
Resources……………………………………………………....153

When purpose is not known, abuse is inevitable.

-Myles Munroe

Introduction

Birthed Into Purpose

I was born on the Third Day, January 3rd…birthed out of waters of the flesh. After many years of wading through the tempering process of life's journey, in January of 1994 I was born a second time; birthed in the Spirit. On August 11th, 2011, I arose and got up from my comfortable sofa in my safe suburban home. I was instructed and directed to my appointed territory, my assignment. On that day I plugged into electricity, I tapped into the current of the supernatural power of God. I was reborn for the third time, birthed into my destined purpose. The birthing place this time was in the deep spiritual waters, depths unknown of God's grace and mercy. Depths so deep that proved the potential for my planned purpose. The purpose that I could not see in the natural was awakened and I could see crystal clear through supernatural eyes and a revived heart that could sense and detect my steps being ordered into my purpose which gave me the ability to move my feet. Our purpose is innate within each of us. We must have our hearts positioned unto Him to recognize it and receive it. When we accept our purpose and calling we become fully alive. Living this life on purpose, conforming to who we were born to be, brings a new confidence and builds an inner strength to fulfill the master plan for our lives! I am thankful for His plan and purpose for my life. Are you ready to discover yours?

I am praying for you as you begin this journey!

Born on purpose,

Dana McCartney Candillo

Jeremiah 29:11

This devotional study guide is designed to be a workbook where you can record your thoughts and respond to what you've read. Each devotional section includes questions and pages where you can write down your initial thoughts as well as notes.

What does a broken girl need to become whole and free in Jesus?

For most, the answer is not "just pray" or "go to church." It's not a "simple fix" although women are always interested in how to improve themselves. What women want to know is "how do I do it?" Specifically, women want to know how to change, identify who they really are on the inside, increase their faith and confidence, and improve their lives.

The world is changing the hearts of people, not only with media but also with voices and noise drawing us into lifestyles and circumstances that appear too glamorous, but often leave women defeated, abused and unloved. The rules are changing, but there is one who remains the same; yesterday, today, and forever- our God. *"and provide for those who grieve in Zion—to bestow on them a crown of beauty instead of ashes, the oil of joy instead of mourning, and a garment of praise instead of a spirit of despair. They will be called oaks of righteousness, a planting of the Lord for the display of his splendor." Isaiah 61:3 NIV.* All hurting women are asking the same questions:

- Am I really valuable?
- Will my life ever change?
- Does God love me?
- Am I too far gone for God's love?
- How did I end up here?
- Why am I so broken?
- Can I be fixed?
- Am I beautiful?

These questions haven't been addressed either by traditional self help books (which still provide surface level information about change for abused women) or by existing "self help guides" (which either focus on introductory basics or on lists of resources). Women are eager for material that will help them heal and be made whole -- material that not only tells them what is available to them in God, but how to restore that which has been lost.

Beauty Before Brittany is designed to answer these questions, and more. It is divided into four sections that correspond with the way most women "experience" their lives: Unlocking the Pain (exploration), Unlocking their Passion (using experiences to gain perspective), Unlocking their Purpose (establishing their foundation for wholeness) and Opening the Door to Destiny (confidence for the future). Each chapter highlights a particular aspect of the woman's pain experience and how that aspect has affected (and can be improved) by trusting God for His design and purpose for her life.

Women will find the Resource Appendix particularly useful. This appendix doesn't simply list resources by name, but divides them into categories and provides a brief description of each one. It focuses upon the use of "tools" – websites, books, music, women's health agencies and more that provide links to help a woman on her journey to maintaining her "whole" life. Visit LionsBeautyQueens.org for other resources including pregnancy crisis and more that can help while still on the journey. If a woman can really be helped by music, resources are shared. If a different woman needs help with kicking old habits, tips are provided on "how to" break addictions.

Beauty Before Brittany is written from the perspective of a woman whose been abused; by life, by people and by the world. It asks the questions hurting women ask, and answers them with the love women need to improve their lives through a relationship with Christ. It dispels many of the myths that have surrounded broken women and demonstrates a host of new opportunities for wholeness in Christ. Dana McCartney Candillo takes women through the process of revealing their pain to discovering their passion and igniting their purpose for 21st century living, God's way. Armed with personal stories, blog entries, and questions that require the courage to dig deep; every woman finds herself restored to their place of *Beauty Before Brittany.*

A Word from the Author

Beauty Before Brittany…Born to be His Beauty Queen

"ALL GIRLS DREAM OF THE FAIRYTALE"

Once upon a time…before Brittany, there was a girl. A beautiful, beloved girl. A precious and innocent little girl. She was a child princess belonging to the greatest King of all Kings. She just did not know it yet. For to her demise she was never treated as royalty but as invisible and shameful. Instead of being deemed worthy she was labeled worthless, powerless and insignificant. Although others placed this belief on her through their corrupt actions, she began to believe their spells of lies. But the King, whose name was Jesus, He knew better. All along He had a perfect royal plan. Jeremiah 29:11 states ***For I know the plans I have for you," declares the LORD, "plans to prosper you and not to harm you, plans to give you hope and a future***. It was a plan to prosper her. A plan to be His heir. A plan of a perfectly designed purpose; His treasure. The plan was so magnificent, it was the masters' plan placed innately within her. She now needed to allow God to show her how to unlock it. The only way of unlocking this treasure was to somehow find that uniquely cut and patterned key. God gives us the key to the kingdom; the key of all keys! ***I will give you the keys of the kingdom of heaven; whatever you bind on earth will be bound in heaven, and whatever you loose on earth will be loosed in heaven."*** Matthew 16:19 NIV It is the only tool that can open the greatest door of your life! That specific key can only be found by searching the heart and soul, life experiences, and ushering in God's powerful all-knowing presence into your life. Jesus holds the key and wants to hand it to you as your will matches up with His. He will trust you with this key in hopes that you will open the door, commune with Him, and put all your gifts and faith into action. Within that action, instructions will be revealed. He will reveal to you

His royal assignment for your life, created and designed specifically tailored just for you. His purpose; uniquely for you.

Before Brittany, the challenges of childhood fogged and blurred the direction and knowledge of the key. The key was to my true purpose. Child abuse, neglect, abandonment, sexual abuse and severe poverty are all painful experiences that lead to wrong and false beliefs. The pain and lies that hide there have the ability to jade decisions and thought processes when a child subconsciously strategizes for survival. These survival strategies involve developing a blueprint of those lies. As a child, many times it can be very difficult and confusing to separate and process behaviors or things that are happening in our immediate surroundings, circumstances trap the child in dysfunction. I will never understand why such evil is allowed to be presented to the life of a child. All I know is that when this child grows up and comes to believe the truth...watch out because that child has grown strong, with increased abilities of awareness to fully walk out purpose and God-assignment with authority and boldness! Pain can create an unrelenting passion and drive that can be channeled and developed to wreak havoc on the kingdom of darkness! Along your path of discovery you may need to revisit your past – not live in it! – to heal and learn what really drives you. This will reveal what you really care about and are charged about. Taking the steps can lead toward discovering your purpose and plan. **Wherefore I say unto thee, Her sins, which are many, are forgiven; for she loved much: but to whom little is forgiven, the same loveth little.** Luke 7:47 KJV

Before Brittany there was beauty, innocence; purity; a set apart (holy) and narrow pathway to Heaven. When we choose to believe Satan's lies, hidden in our pain, the pathway is interrupted. We get away from the guided route, off on a side road that leads to a dead end.

Like many girls with unfortunate pasts and childhoods, I invested time in the dead end. I had no goals or dreams that would be successful; I felt no purpose, no direction, no hope. On that dead end road is where I met "Brittany." I was a big believer in lies. I lived in a world of deception made of false hopes, false promises, and a false illusion about life. Brittany was this powerful, manipulative, surviving force of a girl that I grew into. I became Brittany so that I could bury my childhood, all my mistakes and mishaps. She was my best attempt at breaking all the damage that had been done to me as a child. I desired to forget about all of it, but I could not. By "Becoming Brittany", a successful dancer, locked into the "glamorous life" of the sex industry, I could put on my mask and survive in the circus of my life! I had long forgotten any chance of knowing that little pure princess in the beginning of my story. Her purity was wrecked! Her innocence stolen, mind confused, and her heart was shattered. She had lost hope. Brittany brought a false security and safety, plowing and bulldozing through life at full force. Her lifestyle was a daily survival mechanism. She strived to be the total opposite of all that had been done to her and that she experienced in her life as a child. She knew without drive, she would die. What she didn't know was that she was channeling her drive in the wrong direction! Anything that has breath will go to extreme measures to survive drowning.

For as long as I can remember, I have always been a very driven and focused person. How could I drive in the correct lane ignoring all the warnings, stop lights, directions, safety precautions, green lights and road blocks? Simple…I could not. I was speeding, running red lights, swerving all over the road, wrecking into road blocks and running into other vehicles! I was on a clear path of destruction on my way to crashing and burning. Had God left me or forgotten me? NO. Had I gone and followed my own direction, completely ignoring His ways and His warnings? YES. Survival mixed with self can have the potential to go south fast! A prescription for a slow death. If drugs are mixed with this combination the death may be accelerated, rapid and devastatingly eventful. Ladies, it is time to process the past, break the silence, and to unravel all the lies. It is time to discover real truth. It is time to live again (or for the first time)! Let us begin…let us journey together…and ultimately pass the baton of freedom and grace to the next generation. Run our race…

Let's run with strength and endurance. Let's pass down a new legacy. We were Kingdom Created to live and dance in a Forever Fairytale.

Pain positioned me.

Passion provoked me.

Purpose propelled me!

Unlocking Your Pain

SINKING DEEP By HILLSONG

Standing here in your presence
In a grace so relentless
I am won by perfect love
Wrapped within the arms of heaven
In a peace that last forever
Sinking deep in mercy's sea

I'm wide awake, drawing close, stirred by grace
And all my heart is yours
All fear removed, I breathe you in, I lean into
Your love, oh your love

When I'm lost you pursue me
Lift my head to see your glory
Lord of all, So beautiful
Here in you I find shelter
Captivated by the splendor
Of your face, my secret place

I'm wide awake, drawing close, stirred by grace
And all my heart is yours
All fear removed, I breathe you in, I lean into
Your love, oh your love

Your love so deep, Is washing over me
Your face is all I seek, you are my everything
Jesus Christ, You are my one desire
Lord hear my only cry, to know you all my life

I'm wide awake, drawing close, stirred by grace
And all my heart is yours
All fear removed, I breathe you in, I lean into
Your love, oh your love

Songwriters: JOEL DAVIES, AODHAN KING

Chapter One

Uncover
Revealing Myself for Renewal

**If we confess our sins, He is faithful and righteous to forgive us our sins and to cleanse us from all unrighteousness.
(1 John 1:9 NIV)**

There comes a time in most of our lives when we feel the need to try and "find" ourselves. We ask ourselves that same old question which has been handed down generation after generation. Who am I? What do I want to be? Can I become the *she* I want to be? Am I willing to do the work? Do I want to be free?

For many, this search begins in the early adult years. Having already gone through infancy, childhood, teen trials and becoming an adult … You feel a need to explore your heart, identify what you like and don't like, solidify your beliefs, and once you do, you imagine you'll be able to get on with … life.

During this process, it may seem nobody understands this and during your search for who you are those around you may act as if you are going through some ridiculous unimportant phase. Friends and even family may ridicule you during this soul searching.

Sometimes this desire to search our souls doesn't happen until well into adulthood, which people have dubbed as "going through a mid-life crisis" … The results of this are usually devastating, causing things like infidelity, broken homes, career changes, relocation, the loss and/or respect of your loved ones, etc.

Finding yourself doesn't have to be such a difficult time in your life. The TRUTH is that WHO you are has already been determined. This study can help you to find out who you are without a lot of psychological analyzing and be a positive experience at the same time. Throughout this book you will be challenged, but encouraged to allow God to do a transforming work in you emotionally, spiritually and ultimately physically through His word and being open to change.

In a world governed primarily by emotions, the human world is one necessarily filled with conflict and distress. Life isn't about avoiding pain. It's not even about maximizing pleasure. It's about living your life the way you need to live it. It's accepting the person you are, accepting what you really need, and going after it — no matter how scared you may be to make that leap.

It's about having faith in yourself and believing God can make you all over again. You have one life. It may have been or is currently filled with sadness or happiness, but you now have an opportunity to change its direction.

There may be plenty of things in life that cause us to fear or try to avoid. But uncovering ourselves before our Almighty God isn't one of them. Don't be the girl who regrets not taking the risk; for a better life filled with more love, power and strength than you could ever imagine. Allow yourself to be loved by God in a way that only He can.

The bible, in the book of Genesis shares that we are made in the likeness of God who wants us to imitate Him. *So God created mankind in his own image, in the image of God he created them; male and female he created them Genesis 1:27 NIV.* After

Adam and Eve sinned in the garden of Eden, they were afraid and hid themselves from God because the knew they had sinned. Don't we, to this day, do the same thing? However, now is a good time you can bring yourself to God and not hide any longer.

Together, we will walk through and discover many ways we can reveal our feelings toward God during the journey. As well, understand and change our feelings about ourselves. Your life is going to change; are you ready for it? In the next chapter, we are going to uncover the areas of your life to find liberation, grace and the love of Christ. With this in depth look at who you are, you will be empowered to become the you - you want to be. As you go through this book remember that you are loved by God first and there is nothing that can separate you from His love. As a matter of fact, I think it's important to share this very important passage of scripture to show you, just how much.

In Romans 8:31-39 New Living Translation (NLT) it reads:

Nothing Can Separate Us from God's Love

What shall we say about such wonderful things as these? If God is for us, who can ever be against us? Since he did not spare even his own Son but gave him up for us all, won't he also give us everything else? Who dares accuse us whom God has chosen for his own? No one—for God himself has given us right standing with himself. Who then will condemn us? No one—for Christ Jesus died for us and was raised to life for us, and he is sitting in the place of honor at God's right hand, pleading for us.

Can anything ever separate us from Christ's love? Does it mean he no longer loves us if we have trouble or calamity, or are persecuted, or hungry, or destitute, or in danger, or threatened with death? (As the Scriptures say, "For your sake we are killed every day; we are being slaughtered like sheep."[a]) No, despite all these things, overwhelming victory is ours through Christ, who loved us.

And I am convinced that nothing can ever separate us from God's love. Neither death nor life, neither angels nor demons,[b] neither our fears for today nor our worries about tomorrow—not even the powers of hell can separate us from God's love. No power in the sky above or in the earth below—indeed, nothing in all creation will ever be able to separate us from the love of God that is revealed in Christ Jesus our Lord.

God is aware of who we are, what we've done and He loves us in spite of it all. You can come to God and uncover yourself and He will not hold anything against you. Instead, He will show you how your life can be full and abundant in love, joy, and peace; which money could never buy or satisfy; only God can do that.

As you begin, here are a few things to remember along the journey:
- Tell God your deepest feelings and emotions
- Speak to God as you would your best friend
- Pray to God by talking to him

God can help you with everything you feel and think. He will speak to you when you talk to Him and He enjoys hearing from you in prayer which we will talk about more and more in this book. Your change can start today, Let's begin!

Chapter Two

From Wretched Rags to Royal Riches
Whose mirror are you looking into?

***All of us have become like one who is unclean...
(Isaiah 64:6 NIV)***

Mirror, mirror lie to me
Show me what I want to see
Mirror, mirror lie to me
Why don't I like the girl I see?
The one who's standing right in front of me.
MZM Lyrics

"Mirror, mirror on the wall, who's the fairest of them all?" said the wicked and jealous Queen gazing into her magic mirror. She felt her envy and pride swell as the magic mirror answered, "The daughter of the King, Snow White is the most beautiful of them all." The Queen's heart was evil and she was instantly fueled with a spirit like that of King Saul. *Now the Spirit of the Lord had departed from Saul, and an evil spirit from the Lord tormented him. 1 Samuel 16:14* She was full of contempt and rage toward Snow White, just as Saul transgressed against David. *Saul became even more afraid of him, and he remained David's enemy for the rest of his life. 1 Samuel 18:29 NIV* The Queen's spirit was so evil that she went so far as to request her heart in a box as proof of death! The Queen and Saul both sought and plotted death against the innocent for self-preservation. They served themselves, their titles and crowns. As they both looked into the mirrors of their own life they saw power, position and self-deity, and the spirit that overcame them was so evil that it commanded death for glorifying themselves. *The thief cometh not, but for to steal, and to kill, and to destroy: I am come that they might have life, and that they might have it more abundantly John 10:10 KJV.* He is a Huntsman! A liar with a false fairytale!

Satan's mirror is full of lies, distorted images and torment. If you look into it long enough you will begin to believe falsehoods. It is full of bait and deception. Many lies are embedded painful experiences leading to agreement to self-protect, preserve or to self-glorify. Satan's lies are the same as in the beginning of Genesis. When he tempted Eve with the apple, the forbidden fruit from the Tree of Life, "Eat and you will be like God, full of knowledge." *Preserve and glorify yourself!* Just as the evil queen disguised herself and offered the poisonous apple to Snow White. Not using wisdom and proper discernment Snow White, daughter of a King, found herself unconscious and trapped in a glass coffin! Alive yet barely breathing! It is "sleeping death" that only true love can revive. Eve experienced punishment and separation from God. Satan is full of tricks and disguises and he will use countless schemes and tactics to lure you to look into his mirror of lies. That mirror is a tempter, a false lover, a deceiver, and tormentor. It's a mirror that is distorted and pieced together by broken and jagged pieces of glass. It is a mirror held up by a peddler selling poison!!

In our brokenness we take the bait of these lies and grasp for answers to *fix it*; fix the hurt, fix the pain, and fix the struggles in the reality of our lives. The reality of these hurts come in three common forms for many women.

1. Low self-esteem and worth. Many women have suffered physical and verbal abuse, child abuse and neglect, and sexual abuse. One in four women are sexually abused as children, or assaulted and raped as adults, leaving these woman feeling worthless and dirty. There are Biblical accounts dating back thousands of years as examples of abuse toward women. On one such account David's daughter, Tamar, possibly age 13 or 14) a royal virgin princess, was tricked, betrayed, and raped by her own brother! She felt dirty and shamed, lived a desolate life, hung her head low and no longer felt nor carried herself like a daughter of a great king. She was stripped of her worth and dignity. She piled ashes on her head *So his servant put her out and bolted the door after her. She was wearing an ornate robe, for this was the kind of garment the virgin daughters of the king wore. Tamar put ashes on her head and tore the ornate robe she was wearing. She put her hands on her head and went away, weeping aloud as she went. 2 Samuel 13:18-19 NIV* and no longer lived as a royal princess. Dinah, Jacob's daughter was a very young girl. She was intoxicated, lured, and brought to an isolated place where an older man raped her; stripping her of her virginity and shaming her family. *Now Dinah, the daughter Leah had borne to Jacob, went out to visit the women of the land. When Shechem son of Hamor the Hivite, the ruler of that area, saw her, he took her and raped her. Genesis 34:1-2. NIV*. This trauma ultimately caused a great hatred and division in Jacob's camp, bringing about a deadly battle in which many lives were taken.

2. Value. Some do not feel valued due to parental or emotional neglect. This can lead to a severely diminished sense of lovability and value. This is especially true if parents do not express love properly to their children. Even worse when father's ignore the great responsibility of the father-daughter relationship bond. Most importantly, when the God of Love, Jesus, is not introduced to His daughters. When these strong foundations are not laid firm, it can become a gateway for the enemy to instill lies and corrupt one's self-worth and identity. The well-fathered daughter is also the most likely to have relationships with men that are emotionally intimate and fulfilling. During the college years, these daughters are more likely than poorly-fathered women to turn to their boyfriends for emotional comfort and support and they are less likely to be "talked into" having sex. As a consequence of having made wiser decisions in regard to sex and dating, these daughters generally have more satisfying, more long-lasting marriages. What is surprising is not that fathers have such an impact on their daughters' relationships with men, but that it seems they generally have *more* impact than mothers do. Their better relationships with men may also be related to the fact that well-fathered daughters are less likely to become clinically depressed or to develop eating disorders. They are also less dissatisfied with their appearance and their body weight. As a consequence of having better emotional and mental health, these young women are more apt to have the kinds of skills and attitudes that lead to more fulfilling relationships with men.

An emerging body of research suggests one more way that dads may shape their daughters' mental health and relationships in adulthood: scholars have found an intriguing link between the way daughters deal with stress as adults and the kind of relationships they had with their dads during childhood. For example, undergraduate women who did not have good relationships with their fathers had lower than normal cortisol levels. And people with low cortisol levels tend to be overly sensitive and overly reactive when confronted with stress. Indeed, the low cortisol daughters were more likely than the higher cortisol daughters (who had the better relationships with their dads) to describe their relationships with men in stressful terms of rejection, unpredictability or coercion. Information shared with permission from Institute for Family Studies, Linda Neilson, June 2014-http://family-studies.org/how-dads-affect-their-daughters-into-adulthood/).

3. Purpose. *Where there is no revelation, people cast off restraint; but blessed is the one who heeds wisdom's instruction Proverbs 29:18 NIV.* When we have no confidence in ourselves due to a weak foundation and toxic relational experiences, our purpose is hindered. Life without purpose lacks ambition and drive. It is easier to become complacent, nonproductive and dry. It becomes fertile ground for Satan to tempt a woman towards agreement with lies in her mind. In the movie

Pretty Woman, Julia Roberts, makes this statement "When all we hear is the bad stuff, it becomes easy to believe." When we become deceived by these beliefs and they become our perceived reality, our true purpose is lost. It is disguised by what we think are our only options, resources, and abilities.

Great insight can be gained by looking at the Biblical account of the woman at the well, she was a good example of being caught up and trapped in lies. She went from man to man looking for love and fulfillment, always coming up empty. She went to fetch water at the well in the heat of the day, when other women may have already left, because of her great amount of shame and self-torment. Her burden was heavy. Jesus says, **"Come to Me, all you who are weary and heavy laden and I will give you rest, for my yoke is easy and my burden is light** Matthew 11:28-30 KJV. She must have been overwhelmed with love that day. True Love - as she encountered Jesus, her compassionate and loving Father who showed her the Father's Love. Surely that was her day of breakthrough. In that moment she had to choose whose mirror she wanted to see herself in. Did she want to continue looking into the mirror of the past, filled with the enemy's lies or gaze into the mirror of the God of Truth? The decision was hers that day upon who to trust and what to believe. She chose to believe Jesus and truth and that day she became an instant evangelist! **"Come, see a man who told me everything I ever did. Could this be the Messiah?"** John 4:29 NIV. The same can be said as we look at the biblical account of the woman caught in the act of adultery **They say unto him, Master, this woman was taken in adultery, in the very act** John 8:4 KJV. As she was drug before her accusers; imagine her guilt and shame. She must have been filled with fear, condemnation and judgment.

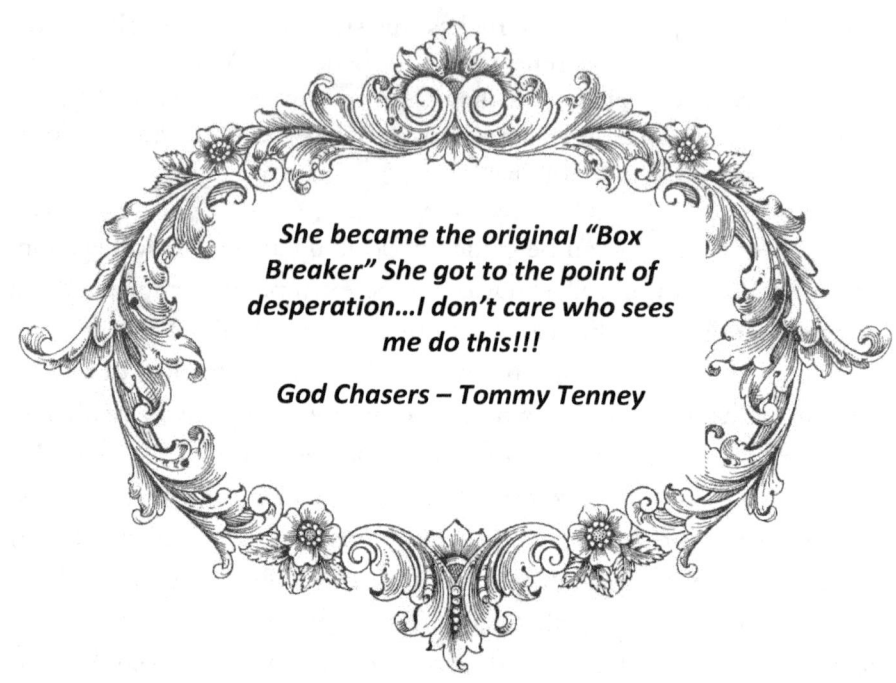

She became the original "Box Breaker" She got to the point of desperation...I don't care who sees me do this!!!

God Chasers – Tommy Tenney

She had been living in lies. Tangled up in a mess, she found herself at the one place she could find truth and forgiveness…the feet of Jesus! **He said, "Whoever has no sin, cast the first stone." The stones fell to the ground, she felt relief and Jesus said, "Woman, where are your accusers now? Go and sin no more."** John 8:11 KJV She had a choice to make that day! Whose mirror would she continue to look into? The famous prostitute in the Bible, Mary Magdelene was filled with lies, evil spirits, confusion and agony. When she met the one and only life giver, Jesus Christ, all that changed, but the decision was hers! She broke her alabaster box! **"A woman came to Him with an alabaster vial of very costly perfume, and she poured it on His head as He reclined at the table** Matthew 26:7 KJV. She washed his feet dried with her hair…forgiven! Whose mirror will you continue to look into Satan's mirror of lies or God's mirror of TRUTH?

Self-Reflection and Journaling

Looking back, are there areas in your life in which you may believe **lies** about yourself? If so, what might some of them be?

_____

_____

_____

_____

_____

_____

_____

She is more precious than rubies; nothing you desire can compare with her. Proverbs 3:15 NIV

Do you believe that you are **valued**? Did you feel valued as a child and do you feel valued as an adult? List some of your childhood experiences & label if each one caused feelings of value or de-value..

_____

_____

_____

_____

_____

_____

_____

_____

_____

And so we know and rely on the love God has for us. God is love. Whoever lives in love lives in God, and God in them. 1 John 4:16 NIV

Do you feel that you are **loved?** What are some of the things that make you feel that you are loved or not loved? There is a difference between knowing the truth and being able to feel/ believe/experience the truth. Did you feel loved as a child? Do you feel loved as an adult?

_____

_____

_____

_____

_____

_____

_____

_____

Are not five sparrows sold for two pennies? Yet not one of them is forgotten by God. [7] ***Indeed, the very hairs of your head are all***

numbered. Don't be afraid; you are worth more than many sparrows.
Luke 12:6-7 NIV

Do you feel that you have **worth**? Are you worthy? Do you feel good about yourself or not? Did you feel that you were worthy or deserving as a child and what experiences create a sense of worth or worthlessness as an adult?

_____

_____

_____

_____

_____

_____

_____

_____

_____

_____

_____

_____

_____

For I know the plans I have for you," declares the LORD, "plans to prosper you and not to harm you, plans to give you hope and a future. Jeremiah 29:11 NIV

Do you believe that your life has *meaning and purpose?* If so, journal what that purpose may be for you. If not, write why not. Journal what experiences drive your *belief that* you are purposed or not. What "idea" or thought "triggers" you to want to *do something* for yourself or others?

_____
_____
_____
_____
_____
_____
_____
_____
_____
_____
_____
_____
_____

In the LORD's hand the king's heart is a stream of water that he channels toward all who please him. Proverbs 21:1 NIV

Is there anything in your life that you hope to *change or improve upon?*

_____

_____

_____

_____

_____

_____

My help comes from the LORD, the Maker of heaven and earth. Psalm 121:2 NIV

What are your **goals and dreams**? List some of the things you would like to do in your life? Now and in the future?

_____

_____

_____

_____

_____

_____

What are some things that could help you to create change and reach your **goals and dreams**?

_____
_____
_____
_____
_____
_____
_____

Jesus answered, "I am the way and the truth and the life. No one comes to the Father except through me. John 14:6 NIV

Have you made a decision for Jesus? Do you have an authentic relationship with Him? Do you have a prayer life? If not, why not start today?

_____
_____
_____
_____
_____
_____
_____

What are your feelings right now about making this decision? Or not? We all have free will and choice.

_____

_____

_____

_____

_____

Salvation Prayer

Dear God in heaven, I come to you in the name of Jesus. I acknowledge to You that I am a sinner, and I am sorry for my sins and the life that I have lived; I need your forgiveness.

I believe that your only begotten Son Jesus Christ shed His precious blood on the cross at Calvary and died for my sins, and I am now willing to turn from my sin.

You said in Your Holy Word, Romans 10:9 that if we confess the Lord our God and believe in our hearts that God raised Jesus from the dead, we shall be saved.

Right now I confess Jesus as the Lord of my soul. With my heart, I believe that God raised Jesus from the dead. This very moment I accept Jesus Christ as my own personal Savior and according to His Word, right now I am saved.

Thank you Jesus, for your unlimited grace which has saved me from my sins. I thank you Jesus that your grace never leads to license sin, but rather it always leads to repentance. Therefore Lord Jesus, transform my life so that I may bring glory and honor to you alone and not to myself.

Thank you Jesus, for dying for me and giving me eternal life. AMEN.

What is God saying to you during your journey?

[1]Prayer is loving communication with God. Prayer is the expression of our inner spiritual needs. Through prayer we can find strength of spirit, guidance, wisdom, joy and inner peace (Psalms 118:5-6, Psalms 138:3, Isaiah 58:9-11, Philippians 4:6-7, 1 Peter 5:7). Prayer may be long or short, alone or in a group, silent or aloud, but it should be a true communication with God and not done for public recognition (Matthew 6:5-8).

God speaks as we are in prayer/ fellowship with Him.

Journal today!
(Feelings, thoughts, reflections)

This is an important time in your life. It's good to take the time and write down how you're feeling on the inside or what God may be speaking to you. This will be a good place to come back to as you watch yourself learn and grow closer to God. It will also be a marker in your life that can be a turning point for you and a faith jolt every time you think back. So, take the time now to write anything and everything you're feeling. Throughout your journey you will be able to stop and reflect on the things you feel changing in your life, your mind, your emotions and your desires.

---

[1] www.christianbiblereference.org

Journal Pages – What Is God saying to You?

Journal Pages - What Is God saying to You?

From the Blog, www.DanaCandillo.com

WELCOME TO THE JUNGLE

Welcome to the Jungle, we take it day by day
If you want it you're gonna bleed but it's the price you pay
And you're a very sexy girl who's very hard to please
You can taste the bright lights but you won't get them for free
~ Guns & Roses ~

I was on a road to destruction, pure desensitization, and a lustful appetite for money that could NEVER be satisfied!~(**SURRENDERED SHOWGIRL**)

Day by Day we have a choice. We make the decisions of which environments to place ourselves into, what roads to take, and which paths to ignore. One day I found myself in a very dangerous jungle, an obstacle course in the wilderness actually. One false move, one lie away, too much alcohol, one night of too many drugs, or any significant weight gain could flood the comparisons and become a game changer instantaneously! A jungle of competition, evil intentions, degradation, false illusions…a world of absolute deceit. Buried in the deep trenches of such a jungle causes one to become visually impaired, compromised in hearing, drained and depleted of one's senses. Thus, caught up in a trap, a snare, so entangled that finding a way out is almost virtually impossible! Captured! Although wicked, the alluring excitement of such a jungle, it's sights, sounds & atmosphere is sheer trickery. And although there is no entry fee, the cost to visit it and the cost to escape it is of a devastating proportion! The Lights & Glamour, the money made hand over fist all begin to fade as truth and reality sets in. No fantasy and/or monopoly of this magnitude exists for free. Before you click on the computer, enter the doors of the commercial sex industry, or choose illusion over reality, will you consider the cost? Will you research the survival rate of this jungle? Can your marriage survive it? Can your family survive it? Are you sure you can survive and escape it? The truth is NO, you won't.

Nothing about this jungle is free. It will cost you guilt, pain, frustration, shame, depression, anxiety, suspicion, PTSD, financial hardship, and dissatisfaction. It's a gamble you will never win. Whether choosing to be an employee or a patron, no one exits unaffected. What daily choices will you make? Will they be choices promoting captivity or freedom? It takes a life of the Lion to conquer the jungle. Conform to Him and live in freedom today!

Unlocking Your Passion

When fear comes knocking at your door, send faith to answer.

-Joyce Meyer

Chapter Three

Gazing Into God's Mirror
New reflections that I see are my daily joy and peace

"Therefore, if anyone is in Christ, he is a new creation. The old has gone, the new has come."
(2 Cor. 5:17 NIV)

The reflection in God's mirror is clear and bright. It shines with truth and true beauty and speaks to your true identity. When you now look into His mirror what do you feel and see that reflects your true identity and who you were created to be? Looking in God's mirror (through His Word and teaching) I can now clearly see new things pertaining to my worth; His purpose and plan for me.
GETTING DOWN TO THE "ROOT" CAUSE

Definition of PRAYER: Prayer is loving communication with God. [2]Again, Prayer is the expression of our inner spiritual needs. Through prayer we can find strength of spirit, guidance, wisdom, joy and inner peace (Psalms 118:5-6, Psalms 138:3, Isaiah 58:9-11, Philippians 4:6-7, 1 Peter 5:7). Prayer may be long or short, alone or in a group, silent or aloud, but it should be a true communication with God and not done for public recognition (Matthew 6:5-8). Important aspects of prayer include:
- Expressions of faith and trust in God
- Confession of our sins
- Praise of God's mighty deeds
- Thanksgiving for all the good things we have received
- Dedication to serve God and other people
- Requests for our needs and the needs of others

---

[2] www.christianbiblereference.org

- Be in Prayer First.
- Seek and Ask the Lord to reveal some things to you that may be painful beginnings or memories of some of the issues that have caused you trouble, stress, pain, depression, anxiety, or any other area of which you may feel stuck. Realize there is always a "why behind the what". Areas where you may feel hindered even years later began and started somewhere by something. It may be possibly an experience, encounter, words, or some type of traumatic event. These circumstances may be where the "root" issue or lies are embedded. Digging down into this will help you Identify the "Root".
- ***Definition of ROOT***: *a* : something that is an origin or source (as of a condition or quality) <*the love of money is the root of all evil* — 1 Timothy 6:10*(Authorized Version)*> the part of a plant that attaches it to the ground or to a support, typically underground, conveying water and nourishment to the rest of the plant via numerous branches and fibers. "cacti have deep and spreading roots" *(Merriam Webster Dictionary, 2016)*

Rooted and built up in him, strengthened in the faith as you were taught, and overflowing with thankfulness Colossians 2:7 NIV. Begin by asking yourself some simple / some hard questions and recalling the answers.

When/Age/Year it began?

_____
_____
_____
_____
_____
_____
_____

What was the environment/your surroundings like at that time?
_____
_____
_____
_____
_____
_____

Who was there for your support?
_____
_____
_____
_____
_____

Who was NOT there for you that you may have thought should have been?
_____
_____
_____
_____
_____
_____

What feelings did you feel/encounter? Examples may be fear, abandonment, lack of trust, lack of attachment, and/or multiple emotions.

_____
_____
_____
_____
_____

What were any or some of the after effects from the situation? Meaning feelings or issues that you feel may have arisen from the incident/s?

_____
_____
_____
_____
_____

Definition of COPING: to struggle or try to manage especially with some success <*cope* with a situation> (Merriam Webster 2016)

What did you do for original coping mechanisms? Meaning, how did you handle or manage those feelings? Do you feel you were coping in healthy ways?

_____
_____
_____
_____

What are you doing today for coping mechanisms? Are they different or the same and do you feel it is healthy for you or you may need to seek and explore new healthier coping strategies?

_____
_____
_____
_____
_____

Definition of TRIGGER: **1**: cause (an event or situation) to happen or exist. 2. A **trigger** in **psychology** is a stimulus such as a smell, sound, or sight that **triggers** feelings of trauma (Psychology Today, 2016).

A Trigger may cause you to think or dwell on past memories, experiences, feelings, and/or actions.

_____
_____
_____
_____
_____

Next, Identify "triggers" and when you have been moved into those moments or patterns of behavior and/or coping mechanisms.

_____
_____
_____
_____
_____

List out your possible triggers and the behavior that is attached to each one.

_____

_____

_____

_____

_____

List out your current coping skills and what you are presently doing for each one of those.

_____

_____

_____

_____

_____

Definition of CHANGE: *a*: to make different in some particular : alter <*never bothered to change the will*>*b* : to make radically different : transform <*can't change human nature*>*c* : to give a different position, course, or direction to (Merriam Webster 2016)

After prayer, reading the Word, wise counsel, support group, education and guidance what do you feel may be more appropriate or additional coping mechanisms and responses that you may replace for the old ones?

_____

_____

_____

_____

_____

Now we can work on "Chopping down the old root and Building a New Root. *They will be like a tree planted by the water that sends out its roots by the stream. It does not fear when heat comes; its leaves are always green. It has no worries in a year of drought and never fails to bear fruit.* Jeremiah 17:8 NIV

- You are now activating positive change in your life! "DO NOT LOOK BACK"! *But Lot's wife looked back, and she became a pillar of salt. Genesis 19:26 NIV*

- Next, we are going to be replacing the old "foundational root" (which are generally embedded with lies and false/condemning self-thought patterns) with a "solid rock WORD root".

- Now, List out these defined old roots and then go directly to the Bible, and look up the most closely matched scriptures pertaining to each issue, feeling, emotion, or event. (*this can be found by looking in the glossary/ back of bible or references for these particular words/things. Or by looking up online.) Once you have these comparisons of truth, apply them right next to each of your listed old roots.

This is what I call building a "TRUTH ROOT".
EX. ANXIETY/*What does God's word say about anxiety?*
See the old root word, next to it write down the scripture (Truth).

LONELINESS/_____

FEAR/_____

REJECTION/_____

OUTCAST/_____

ANGER/_____

BITTERNESS/_____

Before Brittany…Before _____ (Fill in according to former name, abuse, the divorce, the rape, the abortion, the abandonment, the miscarriage, the pain…whatever it is, has been and has had you "stuck"! Pray for God to reveal answers as you reflect on each one. As we journey through this discovery of our true reflection, let's look at and study what God's Word says about how HE sees us. This is the way we overcome the lies of the enemy that have been placed in our souls. God's Word is the infallible, undeniable, never changing TRUTH forever! We must replace lies with TRUTH. This is how we become FREE! So, let's look at some of these lies, labels and/or circumstances and study what the Bible has to reveal to us.

1. Lie: I am a mistake. **TRUTH**: *For You formed my inward parts; You wove me in my mother's womb. 14I will give thanks to You, for I am fearfully and wonderfully made; Wonderful are Your works, And my soul knows it very well.* Psalm 139:14 NIV

What I believe about me and why I am here:

_____
_____
_____
_____
_____
_____

These are some of the lies I had to overcome during transition:

_____
_____
_____
_____
_____
_____

What God says about me and this label? Pray and study the scripture and then write down what you feel about the truth that is revealed to you during prayer time. Do this for each topic listed as follows. What can you believe?

_____
_____
_____
_____
_____
_____

What do you have trouble believing?

_____
_____
_____

_____

_____

2. Lie: My life is ugly and a mess. I am ugly. **TRUTH:** *For we are God's masterpiece. He has created us anew in Christ Jesus, so we can do the good things he planned for us long ago.* Ephesians 2:10

When my father and my mother forsake me, then the LORD will take me up. Psalm 27:10

What I believe/feel:

_____
_____
_____
_____
_____
_____

What God has revealed to me:

_____
_____
_____
_____
_____

3. Lie: I am alone. **TRUTH:** *Be strong and of a good courage, fear not, nor be afraid of them: for the L*ORD *thy God, he it is that doth go with thee; he will not fail thee, nor forsake thee.* Deuteronomy 31:6 KJV

What I believe/feel:

_____
_____
_____
_____
_____
_____

What God has revealed to me:

_____
_____
_____
_____
_____
_____

4. Lie: I've gone too far for God to love me. I've made too many mistakes. **TRUTH:** Seventy times seven, second chances, forgiveness. *Then Peter came and said to Him, "Lord, how often shall my brother sin against me and I forgive him? Up to seven times? Jesus said to him, "I do not say to you, up to seven times, but up to seventy times seven. "For this reason the*

kingdom of heaven may be compared to a king who wished to settle accounts with his slaves. Matthew 18:21-23 NIV

What I believe/feel:

_____
_____
_____
_____
_____
_____

What God has revealed to me:

_____
_____
_____
_____
_____
_____

5. Lie: I'll always live with fears and anxieties. Worry. **TRUTH:** *Do not be anxious or worried about anything, but in everything [every circumstance and situation] by prayer and petition with thanksgiving, continue to make your [specific] requests known to God.* Philippians 4:6 AMP

What I believe feel:

_____
_____

_____
_____
_____
_____

What God has revealed to me:

_____
_____
_____
_____
_____

6. Lie: No one loves me, I am not lovable. **TRUTH:** *For God so loved the world that he gave his one and only Son, that whoever believes in him shall not perish but have eternal life.* John 3:16 NIV **Love never fails**. 1 Corinthians 13:8 KJV

What I believe/feel:

_____
_____
_____
_____
_____

What God has revealed to me:

_____
_____
_____
_____
_____
_____

7. Lie: I can't make it on my own financially. **TRUTH:** *But my God shall supply all your need according to his riches in glory by Christ Jesus.* Philippians 4:19 NIV *Wisdom is a shelter as money is a shelter, but the advantage of knowledge is this: Wisdom preserves those who have it.* Ecclesiastes 7:12 NIV

What I believe/feel:

_____
_____
_____
_____
_____
_____

What God has revealed to me:

_____
_____
_____
_____
_____

8. Lie: No one cares about me, about my situation. **TRUTH:** *The LORD has been mindful of us; He will bless us; He will bless the house of Israel; He will bless the house of Aaron.* Psalm 115:12 KJV

What I believe/feel:

_____
_____
_____
_____
_____
_____

What God has revealed to me:

_____
_____
_____
_____
_____
_____

9. Lie: I am not intelligent or smart enough. **TRUTH** *And he hath filled him with the spirit of God, in wisdom in understanding, and in knowledge, and in all manner of workmanship;* Exodus 35:31 NIV

Wisdom is the principal thing; therefore get wisdom: and with all thy getting get understanding. Proverbs 4:7 NIV

What I believe/feel:

_____
_____
_____
_____
_____
_____

What God has revealed to me:

_____
_____
_____
_____
_____
_____

10. Lie: No one understands me or the pain I'm going through. **TRUTH:** *But emptied Himself, taking the form of a bondservant, and being made in the likeness of men. 8Being found in appearance as a man, He humbled Himself by becoming obedient to the point of death, even death on a cross....* Philippians 2:7-8 NIV

For we do not have a high priest who cannot sympathize with our weaknesses, but One who has been tempted in all things as we are, yet without sin. Hebrews 4:15 NIV

What I believe/feel:

_____
_____
_____
_____
_____
_____

What God has revealed to me:

_____
_____
_____
_____
_____
_____

11. Lie: I am fatherless. **TRUTH: Psalms 68:5** - A father of the fatherless, and a judge of the widows, [is] God in his holy habitation. AMP

1 Peter 1:3 - Blessed [be] the God and Father of our Lord Jesus Christ, which according to his abundant mercy hath begotten us again unto a lively hope by the resurrection of Jesus Christ from the dead, AMP

What I believe/feel:

_____
_____
_____

_____
_____
_____

What God has revealed to me:
_____
_____
_____
_____
_____

12. Lie: I cannot break free from (circle any that apply) drug addiction, alcohol addiction, sexual addiction, depression, anxiety, fear, things in my life that I know are destructive and harmful, abusive relationships, eating disorder, wrong thinking, bad habits, poor decision making, sinful lifestyle behaviors. **TRUTH:** Freedom, break bondage.

If the Son therefore shall make you free, ye shall be free indeed. John 8:36 NIV

For the law of the Spirit of life in Christ Jesus hath made me free from the law of sin and death. Romans 8:2 NIV

It is for freedom that Christ has set us free. Stand firm, then, and do not let yourselves be burdened again by a yoke of slavery. Galatians 5:1 NIV

The WORD of God says: **And the LORD answered me, and said, write the vision, and make it plain upon tables, that he may run that readeth it.** Habakkuk 2:2 NIV

Meditate on these newly replaced "TRUTH ROOTS", Draw them out on paper, write what you now have learned to be true and apply them to your daily thoughts and living. When the old thoughts, patterns, and/or behaviors come your way replace each of these things with the Truth of what you have learned and journeyed through and soon they will take deep root, continue to water them and you will grow in a new found confidence that only the Lord can provide and all the past negativities will have No hold. His Word is brand new every day and shines fresh light on each and every area that we choose to surrender to Him! For a creative reminder place these Truth Roots and new found beliefs (that I pray are now Deep down in your spirit) on a vision board, on your wall, on cards in your car or purse, and anywhere as a helpful reminder that you can reflect upon in times of need and times of weakness. ***Therefore I take pleasure in infirmities, in reproaches, in necessities, in persecutions, in distresses for Christ's sake: for when I am weak, then am I strong.*** 2 Corinthians 12:10 NIV Know and Believe that Jesus is FOR YOU and He is a Truth Teller…..He cannot and will not ever lie. So, hold tight to His Word! Walk in His Word, His Light & His Love!

- Lastly, give yourself GRACE! Know that we are all human and make mistakes and as we are walking through this journey called life we will have setbacks, make mistakes, and occasionally blow it!! When this happens as it will. ***"I have told you these things, so that in me you may have peace. In this world you will have trouble. But take heart! I have overcome the world"*** John 16:33 NIV. Stay calm, and rest assured that you are redeemed and He is the God of second chances or as many as you will Ever need! With this said he also transforms you with plans and purpose. ***And we know that in all things God works for the good of those who love him, who have been called according to his purpose Romans 8:28 NIV and For I know the plans I have for you," declares the LORD, "plans to prosper you and not to harm you, plans to give you hope and a future.*** Jeremiah 29:11 NIV.

The most important thing is that you get back up EVERY time you may fall, Keep your focus on Jesus (Phil. 4:8-9) and begin again……Walk mightily in these Truths, Know Thyself, and Lean into His LOVE Daily *Come unto me, all ye that labour and are heavy laden, and I will give you rest. Take my yoke upon you, and learn of me; for I am meek and lowly in heart: and ye shall find rest unto your souls.* Matthew 11:28-29 KJV

- He will never leave you nor forsake you and His Truth, His Word is a lamp unto our feet. ***Thy word is a lamp unto my feet, and a light unto my path.*** Psalm 119:105 KJV Stay in the Truth ***Stand firm then, with the belt of truth buckled around your waist, with the breastplate of righteousness in place,*** Ephesians 6:14 NIV and it WILL SET YOU FREE!!!

When we finally come to the realization that we truly are "new" and "alive" in Him we experience true peace, freedom, and new found confidence in ourselves. There really is only one way out – His name is Jesus. Without Jesus there is no real rescue! Freedom comes from knowing that His blood, mercy, grace, love and presence is always covering us and that promise is true to the end. No matter what we've done or if we mess up and blow it, we are daughters of the King. A King, a Father who forgives is all encompassing. He will never deny His children grace. Rest in this fact! ***For the LORD God is a sun and shield; the LORD bestows favor and honor; no good thing does he withhold from those whose walk is blameless.*** Psalms 84:11 NIV

Does any unforgiveness remain? If so, list all people/circumstances you need to forgive. Pray and release in forgiveness.

_____
_____
_____
_____

What does it look like today, looking into truth, God's mirror? Can you see a difference in your reflection? Do you see a new you? List a few differences:

_____
_____
_____
_____
_____

I press toward the mark for the prize of the high calling of God in Christ Jesus. Philippians 3:14 NIV

Where are you on your journey? Explain the ease or difficulty level during your time of healing and transformation?

_____
_____
_____
_____
_____

In everything give thanks: for this is the will of God in Christ Jesus concerning you. I Thessalonians 5:18 NIV

Are you thankful for your journey and life? List five things you are thankful for:

_____

_____

_____

_____

What are some areas/things in your life that God has revealed to you or has brought you through in this change process? What are the three most important at this time?

_____

_____

_____

_____

And be not conformed to this world: but be ye transformed by the renewing of your mind, that ye may prove what is that good, and acceptable, and perfect, will of God. Romans 12:2 NIV

How do you feel about your life today as opposed to when you first came into the support group/classes/or began this journey of self-study?

_____

_____

_____

_____

God's mirror is love shining and reflecting on humanity. It is full of compassion and His powerful presence beaming, waiting for each of us to accept it, desire it, and experience it! The Holy Spirit of God desires to be ushered into our hearts and dwell there indefinitely. He desires to continuously hold up the mirror to your life and help you each and every day of your life. When you allow God to live in your heart, He will invade every area that you allow Him to and surrender to Him. He is a gentleman and gives you a free will so you must choose how much you want to shine and reflect for Him. **Be strong and courageous. Do not be afraid or terrified because of them, for the LORD your God goes with you; He will never leave you nor forsake you.** Deuteronomy 31:6 NIV. His love is everlasting and forever unchangeable.

What does Grace look like in your life today?

_____

_____

_____

_____

_____

What does mercy look like in your life today?

_____

_____

_____

_____

_____

What are ways you experience God in your everyday life?

_____
_____
_____
_____

Love Scriptures

John 3:16 - For God so loved the world that he gave his one and only Son, that whoever believes in him shall not perish but have eternal life.

Romans 8:37-39 - Know in all these things we are more than conquerors through him who loved us. For I am sure that neither death nor life, nor angels nor rulers, nor things present nor things to come, nor powers, nor height nor depth, nor anything else in all creation, will be able to separate us from the love of God in Christ Jesus our Lord.

Ephesians 2:4-5 - But because of his great love for us, God, who is rich in mercy, made us alive with Christ even when we were dead in transgressions—it is by grace you have been saved.

Romans 5:8 - but God shows his love for us in that while we were still sinners, Christ died for us.

Zephaniah 3:17 - The LORD your God is with you, the Mighty Warrior who saves. He will take great delight in you; in his love he will no longer rebuke you, but will rejoice over you with singing.

1 Peter 5:6-7 - Humble yourselves, therefore, under the mighty hand of God so that at the proper time he may exalt you, casting all your anxieties on him, because he cares for you.

Psalm 86:15 - But you, O Lord, are a God merciful and gracious, slow to anger and abounding in steadfast love and faithfulness.

I know His mirror is reflective in my life because I see:

_____

_____

_____

I now trust God for these things in my life:

_____

_____

_____

_____

_____

_____

I experience God in my life the most when:

_____

_____

_____

_____

_____

_____

I believe that I am loved! I know God loves me today because:

_____
_____
_____
_____
_____
_____

I know that transformation is a process and when I make mistakes or poor decisions I know I can come to God and not be judged or condemned but loved, accepted, forgiven, and given another chance. **_Great is his faithfulness; his mercies begin afresh each morning._** Lamentations 3:23 NLT

I can use these steps:
- Prayer
- Ask forgiveness, repent
- Start over
- Ask God for clarity in future decision making
- Stay close to the Father!
- Go to the Word of God and spend time in His presence

I know that change is a part of life and we will continue to change and grow. These are positive changes and I see myself growing in the future in these ways:

_____
_____
_____

_____

_____

_____

_____

What God Says about Me Scriptures

I am God's child. *Galatians 3:26*

I am Jesus' friend. *John 15:15*

I am a whole new person with a whole new life. *2 Corinthians 5:17*

I am a place where God's Spirit lives. *1 Corinthians 6:19*

I am God's Incredible work of art. *Ephesians 2:10*

I am totally and completely forgiven. *1 John 1:9*

I am created In God's likeness. *Ephesians 4:24*

I am spiritually alive. *Ephesians 2:5*

I am a citizen of Heaven. *Philippians 3:20*

I am God's messenger to the world. *Acts 1:8*

I am God's disciple-maker. *Matthew 28:19*

I am the salt of the earth. *Matthew 5:13*

I am the light of the world. *Matthew 5:14*

I am greatly loved. *Romans 5:8*

What do I believe about what God says about me?

_____
_____
_____
_____
_____

How can God's mirror help me in decision making?
What does God's Word say regarding my decisions and choices?

_____
_____
_____
_____
_____
_____
_____

Chapter Four

Finding Hope in God
You're Everything I Need

Be strong and take heart, all you who hope in the LORD.
(Psalm 31:24)

In this chapter, I want to share with you the scriptures more intimately here because finding hope in God comes from knowing and abiding in His Word. Most people understand hope as wishful thinking, as in "I hope something will happen." This is not what the Bible means by hope. The biblical definition of *hope* is "confident expectation." Hope is a firm assurance regarding things that are unclear and unknown (Romans 8:24-25; Hebrews 11:1, 7). Hope is a fundamental component of the life of the righteous (Proverbs 23:18). Without hope, life loses its meaning (Lamentations 3:18; Job 7:6) and in death there is no hope (Isaiah 38:18; Job 17:15). The righteous who trust or put their hope in God will be helped (Psalm 28:7), and they will not be confounded, put to shame, or disappointed (Isaiah 49:23). The righteous, who have this trustful hope in God, have a general confidence in God's protection and help (Jeremiah 29:11) and are free from fear and anxiety (Psalm 46:2-3).

The New Testament idea of hope is the recognition that in Christ is found the fulfillment of the Old Testament promises (Matthew 12:21, 1 Peter 1:3). Christian hope is rooted in faith in the divine salvation in Christ (Galatians 5:5). Hope of Christians is brought into being through the presence of the promised Holy Spirit (Romans 8:24-25). It is the future hope of the resurrection of the dead (Acts 23:6), the promises given to Israel (Acts 26:6-7), the redemption of the body and of the whole creation (Romans 8:23-25), eternal glory (Colossians 1:27), eternal life and the inheritance of the saints (Titus

3:5-7), the return of Christ (Titus 2:11-14), transformation into the likeness of Christ (1 John 3:2-3), the salvation of God (1 Timothy 4:10) or simply Christ Himself (1 Timothy 1:1).

The certainty of this blessed future is guaranteed through the indwelling of the Spirit (Romans 8:23-25), Christ in us (Colossians 1:27), and the resurrection of Christ (Acts 2:26). Hope is produced by endurance through suffering (Romans 5:2-5) and is the inspiration behind endurance (1 Thessalonians 1:3; Hebrews 6:11). Those who hope in Christ will see Christ exalted in life and in death (Philippians 1:20). Trustworthy promises from God give us hope (Hebrews 6:18-19), and we may boast in this hope (Hebrews 3:6) and exhibit great boldness in our faith (2 Corinthians 3:12). By contrast, those who do not place their trust in God are said to be without hope (Ephesians 2:12, 1 Thessalonians 4:13).

Along with faith and love, hope is an enduring virtue of the Christian life (1 Corinthians 13:13), and love springs from hope (Colossians 1:4-5). Hope produces joy and peace in believers through the power of the Spirit (Romans 12:12; 15:13). Paul attributes his apostolic calling to the hope of eternal glory (Titus 1:1-2). Hope in the return of Christ is the basis for believers to purify themselves in this life (Titus 2:11-14, 1 John 3:3).

Hope Scriptures

Isaiah 9:7

"Of the increase of His government and peace there will be no end, upon the throne of David and over His kingdom, to order it and establish it with judgment and justice from that time forward, even forever more. The zeal of the Lord of hosts will perform this."

Isaiah 11:9

"They shall not hurt or destroy in all My holy mountain, for the earth shall be full of the knowledge of the LORD as the waters cover the sea."

Jeremiah 29:11

"For I know the thoughts that I think toward you, says the LORD, thoughts of peace and not of evil, to give you a future and a hope."

Daniel 2:44

"And in the days of these kings the God of heaven will set up a kingdom which shall never be destroyed; and the kingdom shall not be left to other people; it shall break in pieces and consume all these kingdoms, and it shall stand forever."

Daniel 12:3

"Those who are wise shall shine like the brightness of the firmament, and those who turn many to righteousness like the stars forever and ever."

Micah 4:4

"But everyone shall sit under his vine and under his fig tree, and no one shall make them afraid; for the mouth of the LORD of hosts has spoken."

Zephaniah 3:17

"The LORD your God in your midst, the Mighty One, will save; He will rejoice over you with gladness, He will quiet you with His love, He will rejoice over you with singing."

Malachi 3:16

"Then those who feared the LORD spoke to one another, and the LORD listened and heard them; so a book of remembrance was written before Him for those who fear the LORD and who meditate on His name."

Matthew 25:21

"His lord said to him, 'Well done, good and faithful servant; you were faithful over a few things, I will make you ruler over many things. Enter into the joy of your lord."

1 Corinthians 2:9

"Eye has not seen, nor ear heard, nor have entered into the heart of man the things which God has prepared for those who love Him."

2 Peter 1:10-11

"Therefore, brethren, be even more diligent to make your call and election sure, for if you do these things you will never stumble; for so an entrance will be supplied to you abundantly into the everlasting kingdom of our Lord and Savior Jesus Christ."

1 John 3:2

"Beloved, now we are children of God; and it has not yet been revealed what we shall be, but we know that when He is revealed, we shall be like Him, for we shall see Him as He is."

Revelation 21:4

"And God will wipe away every tear from their eyes; there shall be no more death, nor sorrow, nor crying. There shall be no more pain, for the former things have passed away."

I now feel that I have hope in these areas of my life:

_____
_____
_____
_____
_____
_____

What hope do I now feel in the God who loves me?

_____
_____
_____
_____
_____

Hope in Christ explained

So what does it mean to have hope in Christ? Part of it means having hope in His promises. He made some incredible promises to His disciples, among them the promise that He would return. In John 14:3 Christ says: "If I go and prepare a place for you, I will come again and receive you to Myself." Christ is coming to rule the earth with the resurrected saints as coheirs (Romans 8:17). This promise is at the core of the gospel message.

Does this give us hope? Do we believe the promises we are reading today?

_____
_____
_____
_____
_____
_____

How futile and empty our physical lives would be if we had no hope of life after death. Many people down through the centuries of human existence have lived with pain, sorrow and unfulfilled dreams. How cruel it would be if this life were all there is!

The Bible is filled with hope: a hope beyond what most have dared to dream. There is a resurrection from the dead. In spite of the dangers of imprisonment and martyrdom, Paul boldly proclaimed the faith we can have that God has something very special in mind for us after this life. He did not have hope in this life *only*. His real hope was for the life beyond this physical existence.

Power & Strength Scriptures

"A wise man is strong, and a man of knowledge increases power." **Proverbs 24:5**

"He gives strength to the weary, and to him who lacks might He increases power." **Isaiah 40:29**

"The angel answered and said to her, 'The Holy Spirit will come upon you, and the power of the Most High will overshadow you; and for that reason the holy Child shall be called the Son of God.'" **Luke 1:35**

"Amazement came upon them all, and they began talking with one another saying, 'What is this message? For with authority and power He commands the unclean spirits and they come out.'" **Luke 4:36**

"All the people were trying to touch Him, for power was coming from Him and healing them all." **Luke 6:19**

"You will receive power when the Holy Spirit has come upon you; and you shall be My witnesses both in Jerusalem, and in all Judea and Samaria, and even to the remotest part of the earth." **Acts 1:8**

"With great power the apostles were giving testimony to the resurrection of the Lord Jesus, and abundant grace was upon them all." **Acts 4:33**

"For I am not ashamed of the gospel, for it is the power of God for salvation to everyone who believes, to the Jew first and also to the Greek." **Romans 1:16**

"For the word of the cross is foolishness to those who are perishing, but to us who are being saved it is the power of God." **1 Corinthians 1:18**

"For the kingdom of God does not consist in words but in power." **1 Corinthians 4:20**

"We have this treasure in earthen vessels, so that the surpassing greatness of the power will be of God and not from ourselves." **2 Corinthians 4:7**

"For the weapons of our warfare are not of the flesh, but divinely powerful for the destruction of fortresses." **2 Corinthians 10:4**

"He has said to me, 'My grace is sufficient for you, for power is perfected in weakness.' Most gladly, therefore, I will rather boast about my weaknesses, so that the power of Christ may dwell in me." **2 Corinthians 12:9**

"That He would grant you, according to the riches of His glory, to be strengthened with power through His Spirit in the inner man." **Ephesians 3:16**

"Finally, be strong in the Lord and in the strength of His might." **Ephesians 6:10**

"For God has not given us a spirit of timidity, but of power and love and discipline. Therefore do not be ashamed of the testimony of our Lord or of me His prisoner, but join with me in suffering for the gospel according to the power of God." **2 Timothy 1:7-8**

"Seeing that His divine power has granted to us everything pertaining to life and godliness, through the true knowledge of Him who called us by His own glory and excellence." **2 Peter 1:3**

"Therefore behold, I am going to make them know—This time I will make them know My power and My might; and they shall know that My name is the LORD." **Jeremiah 16:21**

"'Not by might nor by power, but by My Spirit,' says the LORD of hosts." **Zechariah 4:6**

"For I am not ashamed of the gospel, for it is the power of God for salvation to everyone who believes, to the Jew first and also to the Greek." **Romans 1:16**

"For this very purpose I raised you up, to demonstrate My power in you, and that My name might be proclaimed throughout the whole earth." **Romans 9:17**

"Now may the God of hope fill you with all joy and peace in believing, so that you will abound in hope by the power of the Holy Spirit." **Romans 15:13**

"These are in accordance with the working of the strength of His might which He brought about in Christ, when he raised Him from the dead and seated Him at His right hand in the heavenly places, far above all rule and authority and power and dominion, and every name that is named, not only in this age but also in the one to come." **Ephesians 1:20-21**

"He is the radiance of His glory and the exact representation of His nature, and upholds all things by the word of His power. When He had made purification of sins, He sat down at the right hand of the Majesty on high." **Hebrews 1:3**

"Who are protected by the power of God through faith for a

salvation ready to be revealed in the last time."

1 Peter 1:5

It's not surprising if you'd like to leave a note saying you don't think you can do what God is telling you to do during this next decade.

You may be surprised to hear me say this, but I would agree! If God called you to do it, then you shouldn't be able to do it without him. In fact, if you could do it without him, then it's really not a God-thing.

I know you feel that God is asking you to do something that works against your strengths. But God has called you and that means his strength is working through you and that will make you sufficient for the task.

God's Word says your weaknesses, doubts, and insecurities are no surprise to God. You may try to hide them from others, but you can't hide them from the one who created you.

The truth is, God created you with weaknesses. And, since he's God, he couldn't have made a mistake. Is it possible he created you with weaknesses in order to keep you on your knees before him? With you dependent upon him, you're able to do all things through him who strengthens you (Philippians 4:13–14).

This also means God won't let you use weaknesses as an excuse for not doing what he's asking you to do. If God is calling you to a monumental task, then he'll give you everything you need to complete the task, starting with the Holy Spirit working within you.

My friend, God didn't call other people to this task! He called you and in his strength you can do it. The God-who-loves-you is with you for every step you take as you follow Jesus toward your destiny.

I now feel that I have power in these areas:

_____

_____

_____

_____

_____

_____

I now feel that I have value because?
I feel I am valuable when:

_____

_____

_____

_____

_____

I know that I was born on purpose and for a purpose!
I am learning that my purpose includes, surrounds and is:

_____

_____

_____

_____

_____

Wise Woman Scriptures

Proverbs 19:13

A foolish son is ruin to his father, and a wife's quarreling is a continual dripping of rain.

Proverbs 21:9

It is better to live in a corner of the housetop than in a house shared with a quarrelsome wife.

Proverbs 21:19

It is better to live in a desert land than with a quarrelsome and fretful woman.

Proverbs 31:10

An excellent wife who can find? She is far more precious than jewels.

1 Timothy 3:11

Even so must their wives be grave, not slanderers, sober, faithful in all things.

Proverbs 11:16

A gracious woman gets honor, and violent men get riches.

Genesis 2:18, 22-24

Then the LORD God said, "It is not good that the man should be alone; I will make him a helper fit for him." ... And the rib that the LORD God had taken from the man he made into a woman and brought her to the man. Then the man said, "This at last is bone of my bones and flesh of my flesh; she shall be called Woman, because she was taken out of Man." Therefore a man shall leave his father and his mother and hold fast to his wife, and they shall become one flesh.

Proverbs 31:20-21

She opens her hand to the poor and reaches out her hands to the needy. She is not afraid of snow for her household, for all her household are clothed in scarlet.

Proverbs 31:26

She opens her mouth with wisdom, and the teaching of kindness is on her tongue.

1 Corinthians 11:3

But I would have you know, that the head of every man is Christ; and the head of the woman is the man; and the head of Christ is God.

Ephesians 5:22-23, 33

Wives, submit to your own husbands, as to the Lord. For the husband is the head of the wife even as Christ is the head of the church, his body, and is himself its Savior... However, let each one of you love his wife as himself, and let the wife see that she respects her husband.

Colossians 3:18

Wives, submit to your husbands, as is fitting in the Lord.

Titus 2:2-5

Older men are to be sober-minded, dignified, self-controlled, sound in faith, in love, and in steadfastness. Older women likewise are to be reverent in behavior, not slanderers or slaves to much wine. They are to teach what is good, and so train the young women to love their husbands and children, to be self-controlled, pure, working at home, kind, and submissive to their own husbands, that the word of God may not be reviled.

1 Peter 3:1-2

Likewise, wives, be subject to your own husbands, so that even if some do not obey the word, they may be won without a word by the conduct of their wives, when they see your respectful and pure conduct.

Proverbs 14:1

The wisest of women builds her house, but folly with her own hands tears it down.

I know that I am a royal heir, His Beauty Queen!
I feel priceless and beautiful when: because?

_____

_____

_____

_____

_____

New things I will look for, strive for and expect in any future friendships and relationships:

_____

_____

_____

_____

_____

Ways I can and will love and respect myself:

_____

_____

_____

_____

_____

How can I continue to learn God's plan and direction for my life?
I will resource myself by/ If I feel I'm in a crisis I will:
- Bible Reading/Daily Devotional
- Worship music
- Visual/audio Bible studies
- Accountability Partners/ Friends
- Mentors
- Pastors/ Spiritual Leaders
- Support Groups / Bible studies
- Christian television/radio
- Christian literature
- Surround myself with positive relationship influences

Find a home church. What to look for when deciding upon a home church?

_____
_____
_____
_____
_____
_____

What tools will I use and resource when I feel I may be struggling and in a battle?

_____
_____
_____
_____
_____
_____

How can I focus, be courageous, and remain steadfast during times of trouble?

___

Crisis question
These are people and places I can count on and go to:
#1 GOD

___

Therefore if any man be in Christ, he is a new creature: old things are passed away; behold, all things are become new.
2 Corinthians 5:17 KJV Today I am Free, healed, whole, new, refreshed. I am revived and alive!

What do I want to do next in my life?

___

_____
_____

What are your new goals since beginning this journey?

_____
_____
_____
_____
_____

Where do you now see yourself in the next five years?

_____
_____
_____
_____
_____

I am giving myself permission to dream again, and to chase after those dreams.

Today I am dreaming about:

_____
_____
_____
_____

I have grown in ways that I feel I may be able to help someone else. Those areas are:

_____
_____
_____
_____
_____
_____
_____

For all have sinned and fall short of the glory of God, Romans 3:23 NIV. What are some mistakes I've made in the past?

_____
_____
_____
_____
_____
_____
_____

What did I learn through them?

_____
_____
_____
_____
_____
_____

What will I do next time?

_____
_____
_____
_____
_____

Reminder!
As you begin to write down your thoughts, and reflections. Seek God in prayer. He will bring to your remembrance things to jot down as you continue on your journey.

Journal today!
(Feelings, thoughts, reflections)

This is an important time in your life. It's good to take the time and write down how you're feeling on the inside. This will be a good place to come back to as you watch yourself learn and grow closer to God. It will also be a marker in your life that can be a turning point for you and a faith jolt every time you think back. So, take the time now to write anything and everything you're feeling. Throughout your journey you will be able to stop and reflect on the things you feel changing in your life, your mind, your emotions and your desires.

Journal Pages - What Is God saying to You?

Journal Pages - What Is God saying to You?

From the Blog www.DanaCandillo.com

THE VOICE

It is up to us to listen and hear. Just then I heard that "still small voice" saying to me, "Get out of here! You do not belong here; this is not for you…Do Not Return"! **(SURRENDERED SHOWGIRL)**

That Voice…soft, quiet, and still. It is so simple & surreal…dreamlike but so real. If we position ourselves to hear from Heaven, Jesus surely speaks. His voice is clear & concise and will orchestrate and lead the way. Its tone is peaceful and gentle yet so Powerful and Directive. So many times in my life I was relying on it and did not even know it! If we've know Him, He never leaves. Even in the midst of trials, mistakes, poor decisions, times of trouble, and steering off track, He is big enough to keep us! Even then, He is still speaking….it's up to us to listen. In my most difficult times when I was sinking deeper and deeper that voice was **Still** there. At times I tried to avoid it, thinking I could figure it all out myself. After all, I was the one running. So Many times just as I was about to make the greatest mistakes and worst decisions that could've changed the course of my life Forever…that Voice got louder. It eventually got louder and louder as I was reaching the point of desperation and reached a point in the wall that I could no longer climb. I didn't need a hand out, I needed a helping hand! That still small voice reached the depths of my soul and extended a hand of **Grace** that no one else has the capability to offer! It transformed my mind, heart, & soul. It has caused me to chase after the wind to find it. It is a Must Have. That voice is what is meant & needed to breathe. Without it, who can find real direction or destiny? He will lead us to Purpose. I am always listening for it, now I **Know** it. When I stand at the edge of the Ocean, It is Crystal Clear. Who's voice are you listening to today? Who are you trusting?

Dana

OCEANS by HILLSONG UNITED

You call me out upon the waters
The great unknown where feet may fail
And there I find You in the mystery
In oceans deep
My faith will stand
And I will call upon Your name
And keep my eyes above the waves
When oceans rise
My soul will rest in Your embrace
For I am Yours and You are mine

Your grace abounds in deepest waters
Your sovereign hand
Will be my guide
Where feet may fail and fear surrounds me
You've never failed and You won't start now

So I will call upon Your name
And keep my eyes above the waves
When oceans rise
My soul will rest in Your embrace
For I am Yours and You are mine

Spirit lead me where my trust is without borders
Let me walk upon the waters
Wherever You would call me
Take me deeper than my feet could ever wander
And my faith will be made stronger
In the presence of my Savior

Oh, Jesus, you're my God!
I will call upon Your name
Keep my eyes above the waves
My soul will rest in Your embrace
I am Yours and You are mine

Songwriters: JOEL DAVIES, AODHAN KING

Unlocking Your Purpose

When God calls you to do something, He prepares you in advance.

-Jentezen Franklin

Chapter Five

Discovering Your "True Reflection"
Restoring the Broken Glass

He healeth the broken in heart, and bindeth up their wounds. (Ps 147:3 KJV)

The "Love" of God can and will restore the broken hearts. If we invite Him He will enter our deepest wounding experiences. He is the mender of the broken and His specialty is restoration. He created you and me, therefore He holds the "owner's manual" for all of the repairs! When the mirror of truth is shattered, it becomes a mirror of Satan's lies. It becomes so distorted, the real you, can longer be seen. **The thief cometh not, but for to steal, and to kill, and to destroy: I am come that they might have life, and that they might have it more abundantly.** John 10:10 KJV In everything I grasped for to seal the brokenness, NOTHING proved to recreate and resolve all the cracks and destruction resonating in the mirror! When using the right "super glue" Jesus Christ revealed in God's Word – who is truth, those jagged pieces of glass can mold and fit back together again. One piece at a time the blurriness becomes clear. As each piece comes together it will grow you stronger than ever before. Your true reflection will shine bright transforming and becoming whole, healthy, and vibrant! Often times we are one decision away from creating change and shifting the direction of our entire lives. When I made the decision to listen to the enticing lies, deception and lure of money, my life changed. Ultimately I found myself searching… I was looking into a mirror of shattered glass and trying to figure out a way to fix it…to fix me.

Only when I searched God's Word for the full and complete truth of my true reflection and identity did my vision return. Then I was able to hold up the mirror for myself and look into it with confidence and real knowledge of myself. God's mirror will tell you who you ARE. It only shines truth and grace. It is a life GIVER. It is a mirror that says you are washed, clean, "White as Snow."

Within those moments of that decision (agreement upon agreement with the enemy), I became someone else, someone lost, a girl I had never known. The brokenness became such tiny fractured pieces of glass that eventually I felt unrecognizable. During all those seven and one half years, I felt I had no power to fix it. I was in control of me and all my decisions, or so I thought…actually being controlled by a puppet master. With emotions mastered, my decisions were based on lies that were deeply embedded and that I believed about myself. When I finally made the decision to allow the light of Jesus to shine into the broken empty hole in my heart, it quickly and intensely spread and filled up all the gaps. When that happened and I began to look into the mirror of broken glass, the cracks and distorted image began to fill up and smooth out. It may not happen quickly for every person. Gradually, I saw a restorative process and began to see a girl whose transformation became apparent. I began to like and appreciate what I was seeing. As I became "new" my true reflection began to result in self-esteem and confidence. Truth will always replace lies and mend the broken *He heals the brokenhearted and binds up their wounds Proverbs 147:3 NIV*. I was seeing my reflection with clarity and wellness. The most profound question is *how do you get from here to there?* How do you like yourself again? How do you better yourself and your life? And how do you become free in many areas of your life including decision making? Transitions and transformations are not always easy, change can be scary. It will take work on our behalf but with God, all things are possible!!! ***And Jesus looking upon them saith, With men it is impossible, but not with God: for with God all things are possible. Mark 10:27 KJV*** You can achieve your desires and dreams. You can become the woman that God designed and created for you to be. Most of all, you can *know and experience that your past does **not** determine your future!* The pains caused by all your wounds God wants to heal; to recover. He restores us to who we were originally meant to be! We must get down to the CORE of who we are (TD Jakes). Our true identity, purpose and plan. Before the abuse, the death, the molestation, the rape, the divorce, the beating, the miscarriage, the loss. He brings us back to purity, wholeness, wellness, and a child-like faith. Are there wounds in your life that you feel God wants to heal and restore? Are you willing for the process to begin?

Faith is taking the first step even when you don't see the whole staircase.

– Martin Luther King, Jr.

Then he had another dream, and he told it to his brothers. "Listen," he said, "I had another dream, and this time the sun and moon and eleven stars were bowing down to me."
Genesis 37:9 NIV

Since you started this journey have your **dreams and goals changed?** What makes you most happy? How do you see yourself fulfilling those dreams and goals? List three to five short term (months/year) goals.

_____
_____
_____
_____
_____
_____

Where there is no vision, the people perish: but he that keepeth the law, happy is he. Proverbs 29:18 NIV

Where do you see yourself in the long term, the next 10 years?

_____
_____
_____
_____
_____
_____

My process of getting back to my CORE self:
What do I truly believe now about my true authentic self?

_____
_____
_____
_____
_____
_____

The LORD is near to the brokenhearted And saves those who are crushed in spirit. Psalm 34:18 NIV

Are there wounds in your life that seem like broken glass – shattered bits and pieces of broken dreams, plans, and unresolved pain? What are those wounds that you would like to allow God to restore and put back together?

_____
_____
_____
_____
_____
_____
_____
_____

Do not be misled: "Bad company corrupts good character."
1 Corinthians 15:33 NIV

Are there memories and/or people in your life who have a negative effect or influence on your behavior and choices?

_____
_____
_____
_____
_____
_____

And when you stand praying, if you hold anything against anyone, forgive them, so that your Father in heaven may forgive you your sins. Mark 11:25 NIV

How has the world hurt you? Have you forgiven them?

_____
_____
_____
_____
_____
_____
_____
_____

How have people hurt you? Have you forgiven them?

_____
_____
_____
_____
_____
_____
_____
_____

Jesus turned and saw her. Take heart, daughter," he said, "your faith has healed you. And the woman was healed at that moment. Matthew 9:22 NIV

What would wholeness look like to you now?

_____
_____
_____
_____
_____
_____
_____
_____
_____

What are your core beliefs, feelings, behaviors, passion, and drive now?

_____
_____
_____
_____
_____
_____
_____
_____

And God saw everything that he had made, and behold, it was very good. Genesis 1:31 NIV

What would you like to see when you look in the mirror?

_____
_____
_____
_____
_____
_____
_____
_____

I can do all things through Christ which strengtheneth me.
Philippians 4:13 NIV

Do you believe you can attain your goals, dreams, and have victory in your life now?

_____
_____
_____
_____
_____
_____

If so, what is one thing you can do *today* to start the process? List some actions you can take now.

_____
_____
_____
_____
_____
_____

Casting all your care upon him; for he careth for you.
I Peter 5:7 NIV

Do you believe in Jesus Christ as your personal Savior? Do you believe that He has the power and authority to help you and heal you through your process? Will you trust Him with your life?

Do you see changes in your life now? How do you feel about what you see?

By creating these changes in your life now do you see how your family, your children, will be better in the future?

List some actions you've taken now as part of this journey:

_____
_____
_____
_____
_____

You have been on this journey and God is helping you change and you're seeing change in your life. This next section helps you to see the lies you may have believed before, but gives you room now to share how the truth has set you free. Take this time now to see all that has been undone from a past in pain and made beautiful by the truth of God.

What I believe/feel now that I've went through this journey and studied biblical truths to apply to my life:

_____
_____
_____
_____
_____

What God has revealed to me:

_____
_____
_____
_____
_____

I experience joy and peace when:

_____
_____
_____
_____
_____

My behavior has changed in these ways:

_____
_____
_____
_____
_____

My choices and decision making are made clearer by:

_____
_____

_____

_____

_____

_____

My dedication to the Lord and continuing to learn, study and be fed looks like:

_____

_____

_____

_____

_____

_____

I can and will focus my mind and heart daily to grow and move forward by praying, reading, support systems, church. This for me looks like:

_____

_____

_____

_____

_____

_____

God's mirror is full of grace and mercy. It's radiant and bright and illuminates the interior deep within the soul. It shines and reflects in the darkest places. All that is brought forth to the light can become transparent and open, no longer to linger in the darkness and secret places of shame.

Journal Pages - What Is God saying to You?

Journal Pages - What Is God saying to You?

From the Blog, www.DanaCandillo.com

A NEW THING

HE makes All things "NEW"! (He who was seated on the throne said, "I am making everything new!" then he said, "Write this down, for these words are trustworthy and true." Revelation 21:5 NIV)…..Likewise when we look into the human heart and begin to strip away the entire hardened exterior, beneath all of the pain and scars from life, lays the protected original and unique state, tender, soft, and pliable. When the true condition is exposed and vulnerable; it then is ready to be molded and shaped in truth by the Potter's hand. Once again it becomes fully ALIVE! **(SURRENDERED SHOWGIRL)**

With this New Year, are you ready for God to do a "New Thing" in your Life? What is that one thing that you have been putting off, dreaming about, praying about, and waiting for? God wants to do a new thing in your life! Are you ready and willing to participate? It will most likely involve getting up off of the sofa! Getting out of your comfort zone, saying Yes and setting your feet in motion! We have to move along side of God. Do not allow the delay of fear or intimidation to hold you back any longer! Fear & Intimidation are not of God! If God has called you to do something "out of the box"…Just do it! Don't worry about thoughts of others…people fear what they do not understand and/or do not want to learn about. Whatever God's plan & purpose is for your life ~ it is Yours! If He has something New for you to do then He will not fail you! It is better to be obedient and try and experience His plan of Glory than to ultimately live in regret with the thoughts of never knowing what you may have missed out on! Just remember whatever the Past holds…it is the PAST!…..Your future is awaiting…Find YOUR Purpose & Arise, Come Alive Now!

~Dana

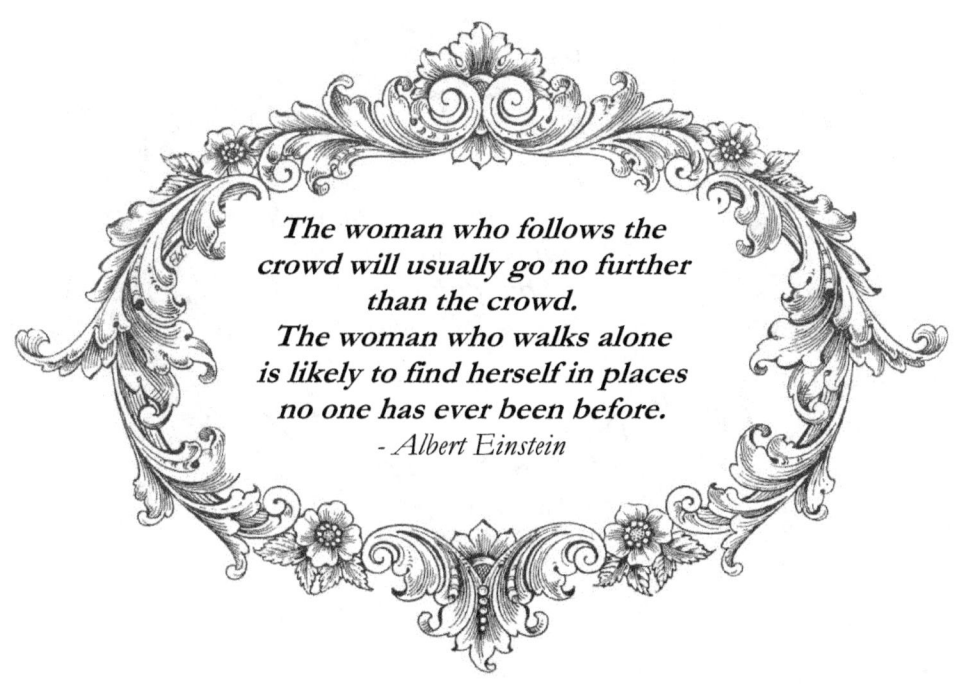

The woman who follows the crowd will usually go no further than the crowd.
The woman who walks alone is likely to find herself in places no one has ever been before.
- Albert Einstein

Power is the most powerful when it is given to somebody who didn't have any.
- T.D. Jakes

Chapter Six

Seeing Me the Way God Sees Me
"Mirror, Mirror"

Therefore, if anyone is in Christ, the new creation has come: The old has gone, the new is here!
(2 Corinthians 5:17 NIV)

Many people ask themselves, "What is God's will for my life?" I've asked this many times. We want to know why we are on earth. We desire to know our unique purpose.

William Barclay says, "There are two great days in a person's life—the day we are born and the day we discover why." It's the "why" that gives us a mission. It's understanding the "why" that sets our feet in motion as we work to live up to our God-given potential.

The why of our existence starts with the heart. "Keep your heart with all diligence, for out of it spring the issues of life," we read in Proverbs 4:23.

Want to know why a man does what he does? Look at his heart. As I learned as a child, "What goes in is what comes out." And what comes out explains a lot about what we believe about what our purpose is in life.

Many times when we are seeking God's will, we want to know what He wants us to do as individuals. And even greater than that, He wants us to know what He has already done and what He desires to do in the next generation.

Henry Blackaby says, "You need to see the heart of God. What has God always been looking for? Then, what does God look for when

He comes to your life? What is He looking for in our generation? Does any of this match your life—not because you say it does, but because God has confirmed it Himself?"

As I thought about this, I realized that for all generations, God's heart has desired a few things:

- Faithfulness in His followers

- Men and women to raise their children in righteousness (right living)

- His Word—truth—to go out to the nations

God's will for my life will line up with His will for the world. The "why" behind "why I was born" will line up with God's "why" for every believer.

This makes me think of my own life. As a servant of God, I am called to understand His heart for all generations. And I am called to listen and obey to my part in seeing His will come to pass.

God spoke of this type of calling for His prophet and priest Samuel: "Then I'll establish for myself a true priest. He'll do what I want him to do, be what I want him to be. I'll make his position secure and he'll do his work freely in the service of my anointed one" (1 Sam. 2:35, MSG).

Many times we want to know God's will so we can set to work at tasks for God. We think of it like getting a homework assignment: "Do this, this and this, and you're good to go."

Instead, God's will is following God's heart. It's allowing God to fill us and work through us, moment by moment. This might look differently throughout our lives. Sometimes we call this "seasons of service." But even though the outward expression of how we are to love and serve others changes, the focus really is loving and serving as an outpouring of God in us.

God didn't give me a list of marching orders to check off. Instead, I've dug into His Word and have grown in my relationship with Him. As I've understood His heart, I've served Him in the ways He's brought before me, for His glory. It's saying yes to what's on His heart as He reveals it to me.

What I do comes out of who I am as a child of God.
Who I am comes out of where my heart is.

Where my heart is depends on how lined up I am with where God's heart is.

I discover God's heart when I read His Word, surround myself with His fellow servants and love and serve those around me who need His love and grace.

Where does this leave me? I cannot be proud of the things I do—of being a mom or an author or a mentor. Instead, it leaves me humble that God has chosen to love and serve through me. Instead, it continually takes me to my knees as I pray and ask Jesus to line up my heart with His.

What is God's will for your life? You'll discover the answer by first asking, "What is God's will?" and then by connecting with Him—in His Word, through prayer and through fellowship with other believers. It's only then that you'll follow His will in what He wants you to do and who He wants you to be today.

Open the Door to Your Destiny

The journey – it took all that to get me here!

-TD Jakes

Chapter Seven

Daughter of the King
Hold His mirror for the Broken

But I have prayed for you, Simon, that your faith may not fail. And when you have turned back, strengthen your brothers."
(Luke 22:32 NIV)

What is my greatest fear? Fears?

What if_____

Then_____

What if_____

Then_____

Most of the time the "what if" is fueled by anxiety and worry straight from the enemy to keep us from moving forward. It is very rare that the "what if" ever amounts to the thoughts and concerns that the mind has escalated the consumptions of thoughts to be. God does not want us to be bound by fear. Fear will only cause your mind and heart to race, stop you in your tracks, and immobilize you from moving forward. If you are stopped you cannot move with purpose and force to accomplish your purpose and calling. We all have a calling to ministry. We each can minister the love of God in our own way. Remember His dream is greater than your dream? If we want to use the life we've been given, the tools we've learned, the grace and mercy that have been bestowed upon us and share all of this with others, we must move past our fears! Replace fears with boldness and confidence in order to hold up God's mirror for someone else! Your testimony, your story, and your love will shine a beautiful reflection for someone else! It will give another woman hope!

Overcoming Fear Scriptures

Psalm 23:4

Even though I walk through the valley of the shadow of death, I will fear no evil, for you are with me; your rod and your staff, they comfort me.

Isaiah 41:13

For I am the Lord, your God, who takes hold of your right hand and says to you, Do not fear; I will help you.

Exodus 14:13

Moses answered the people, "Do not be afraid. Stand firm and you will see the deliverance the Lord will bring you today. The Egyptians you see today you will never see again."

Deuteronomy 31:6

Be strong and courageous. Do not be afraid or terrified because of them, for the Lord your God goes with you; he will never leave you nor forsake you.

2 Timothy 1:7
For God gave us not a spirit of fear; but of power and love and a sound mind.

Luke 1:30

The Lord is my light and my salvation--whom shall I fear? The Lord is the stronghold of my life--of whom shall I be afraid? (Psalm 27:1) But the angel said to her, "Do not be afraid, Mary, you have found favor with God."

Luke 2:10
But the angel said to them, "Do not be afraid. I bring you good news of great joy that will be for all the people."

Hebrews 13:6

So we say with confidence, "The Lord is my helper; I will not be afraid. What can Man do to me?"

John 14:27

Peace I leave with you; my peace I give you. I do not give to you as the world gives. Do not let your hearts be troubled and do not be afraid.

What are some things I can do to get past my fears?
_____
_____
_____
_____
_____
_____

What are some things I can do to build my confidence and be brave and bold for God?
_____
_____
_____
_____
_____
_____

What are some ways I can shine my light and reflection for others?

_____
_____
_____
_____
_____

What are some ways I can share my story and testimony?

_____
_____
_____
_____
_____

"Pain Relates to Pain"....Your Real Life Journey aka "your testimony" will help someone else! As we become overcomers we will be able to pass the baton with helpful insights of learning and discovery of the powerful mysteries of suffering yet carrying our cross with wisdom and divine revelation of pain knowing that pain also has the power to produce love, respect, forgiveness, relatability and propel pulpits to extend mercy and grace and reach the unreachable, the sick , the lost, and the seeking. Quite possibly this may be why God says before we can be fully used we must be broken and crushed. **The LORD is close to the brokenhearted and saves those who are crushed in spirit.** Psalm 34:18 NIV. As mentioned earlier it is clear that there will be pain, trouble, and suffering in this world...no matter how hard we may try, we cannot escape it. So the most important element is HOW we choose to handle it, HOW we choose to Do Life, and Ultimately WHAT we choose to do with HIS SON?

What will you choose to do with His Son? *It would have been better for them not to have known the way of righteousness, than to have known it and then to turn their backs on the sacred command that was passed on to them.* 2 Peter 2:21 NIV

_____
_____
_____
_____
_____

What are some ways, creative ideas, or areas of interest in which I may choose to reach out and help others

_____
_____
_____
_____
_____

How might My Story Relate to others? What ways might I incorporate my journey of experiences into examples of helpful tools for others?

_____
_____
_____
_____
_____

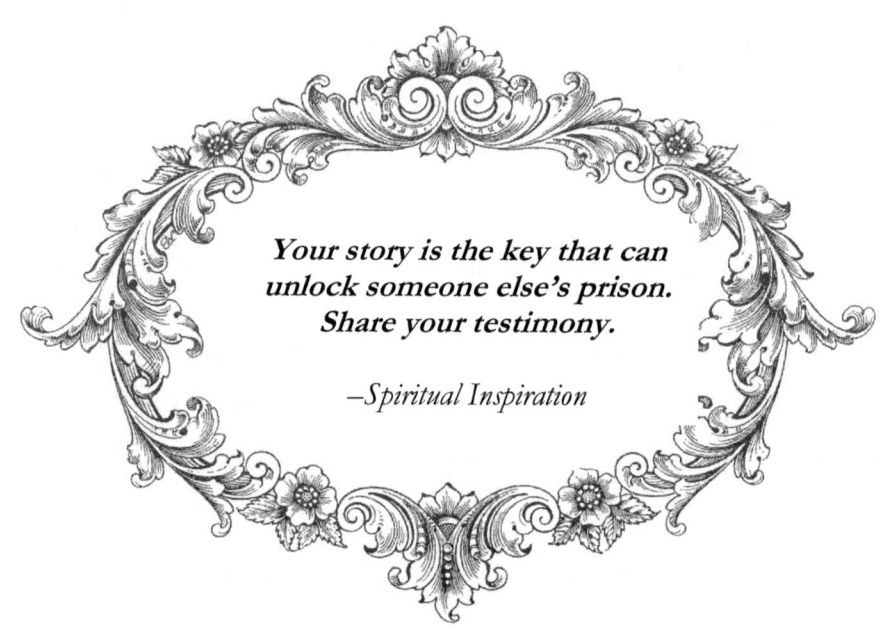

Your story is the key that can unlock someone else's prison. Share your testimony.

—Spiritual Inspiration

Chapter Eight

It's Time
Writing Your Personal Story

**The Lord gave the word:
great was the company of those that published it.
(Psalm 68:11 KJV)**

These days everyone's talking about writing your story. Not just any old story, but the story of your life, the road map that got you to where you are today. For most of us that's a pretty daunting thought. I mean, why would anyone be *interested* in hearing our story anyway?

Life changing

Well, I'm a big proponent of this personal story writing business, and I'll tell you why: **it changed my life.**
I used to be afraid to write, especially about sharing my personal life. I was hiding in my safe comfort zone and warming the bench. But then my ministry led me into writing for therapy in journals and blogs. I could share my personal story, and I found myself feeling good about the transformation that I could see from where I started to where I am today.

I actually had no interest in sharing my story—at first. I thought my past was empty and depressing. But given my role now as both an author and ministry leader, I knew my story was relevant and God wanted to use it.

Resistance

So I sat down in my kitchen and began journaling all my raw thoughts, experiences, emotions and with absolute resistance I began to write the truth of my life. I was full of fear—afraid to reveal my authentic self and the vulnerability that came with doing it. I was also fearful that no one would care about my story. But then it hit me and made sense to me that my story was full and I was able to relate to others!

Daily I began to spend hours by myself at different opportune times and filled multiple journals, pouring out my soul. It all became "real" and eventually I realized that the book, my story, was the place that became the compartment that could hold all the pain and memories in an important place to rest as well as be used. But this time I no longer wrote from a place of resistance, I wrote from the heart.

The result was tears, not just on my part, but my family too.

But more important than the tears was the overwhelming sense of release. In reconnecting with my story I somehow gave it a voice. I gave myself a voice that needed to be heard. Laying all this down lifted bricks and burdens off my shoulders and heart. I no longer had to carry it all. As the words transferred onto the paper, I was assured it would ALL help someone else!

I have continued to write my story and to pursue the practice of helping others do the same. Not only do I believe that telling our stories is an important way to get to know ourselves and find healing, I also believe it's a way to connect with others on a deeply authentic level.

Where do we begin?

Writing our personal stories is the most vulnerable kind of writing we can do. We fear being laughed at, rejected, or that our words will be met with silence. And in turn, we ourselves remain silent.

Through this process I have found six important steps to be helpful:

1. Tap into your emotions.

Your story won't resonate with others if it is void of emotion, as I discovered when writing that first draft of my own story. So take out your paper and pen and write down some key feelings that you associate with your life so far. Then write something about each feeling and the story behind it.

2. List the turning points.

People often make the mistake of starting with their earliest childhood memory and moving through their story chronologically. But rather than starting at the beginning, it's more helpful to make a list of your life's key turning points—those times when you were standing at a crossroads and the direction you chose marked a significant change in your life.

3. Write everything down.

It might not seem like much at the time but it's amazing how one memory leads to another and allows you to go deeper into your story. As with all writing, you may not use many of the scenes you write, but that doesn't mean they don't have a purpose.

4. Use the senses.

The one thing that will help you explore long forgotten memories is to use your senses. As you recall events, try to remember the smells, tastes and sounds that accompany them. Not only will this help you remember details, it will also enrich your writing.

5. Find the theme.

Once you have compiled a large number of significant scenes, it's likely you will begin to see a theme emerging. Your theme is the central question driving your story. The ability to carry this theme through the sequence of events you have recorded is what will turn your individual scenes into one story. It may be that you discover more than one theme. That's okay; it's likely there will be one that stands apart from the others.

6. Tell a story.

You have your theme and a multitude of scenes; you've gone through a box of tissues in the process of exploring your emotions, but have you told a story? As you begin to work on pulling it all together, focus on the person you're sharing the story with. What about your story will connect with him? The best stories are ultimately those that connect with the reader the most.

This process of telling your story is, I believe, one of the most rewarding and clarifying things you can do for yourself, and for others.

So step into that place of discomfort and write the words that will bring freedom and meaning to your life. The time is now! Let your writing begin today...

Journal Pages - Write Your Story

Journal Pages - Write Your Story

Journal Pages - Write Your Story

Journal Pages - Write Your Story

Journal Pages - Write Your Story

Journal Pages - Write Your Story

Journal Pages - Write Your Story

Journal Pages - Write Your Story

Journal Pages - Write Your Story

Journal Pages - Write Your Story

Journal Pages - Write Your Story

Journal Pages - Write Your Story

Journal Pages - Write Your Story

Journal Pages - Write Your Story

Journal Pages - Write Your Story

Journal Pages - Write Your Story

Journal Pages - Write Your Story

Journal Pages - Write Your Story

Journal Pages - Write Your Story

From the blog www.DanaCandillo.com

FROM PAIN TO THE PULPIT

PAIN POSITIONED ME, PASSION PROVOKED ME, PURPOSE PROPELLED ME ~ Dana McCartney-Candillo

I remember trying to drive my old, junky car away from his house. I was gasping for air, I could not breathe. I had lost the only good thing in my life, the love of my life, my heart. I can say this is the closest I ever felt to being suicidal. I drove hysterically to an old friend's house; reverting to my old self-searching for drugs to numb this intense pain. I was in so much pain. I could not lift my head.
~SURRENDERED SHOWGIRL

When the Pain is so great, we are motivated to create change! It is no longer negotiable! We will pursue relentlessly! Do you want to be made well? The Greatest Example that I can apply is the story found in scripture of the man at the pool of Bethesda. John 5:6-9 says, When Jesus saw him lying there and learned that he had been in this condition for a long time; he asked him, "Do you want to get well?" "Sir, the invalid replied," I have no one to help me into the pool when the water is stirred. While I am trying to get in, someone else goes down ahead of me." Then Jesus said to him, "Get Up! Pick up your mat and walk." At once the man was cured; he picked up his mat and walked.

When we are hurting, this is what we may believe about ourselves; that we cannot take steps on our own toward the pool of water. We may feel feelings such as devalued, unloved, disconnected, rejected, alone, helpless and powerless. Can we ask the Lord, What do you say about me? How do you see me? As we begin to answer these questions, can we embrace our truth? Can we Embrace Grace? Friends, pain is like a double-edged sword. It can be a catalyst for Change! Pain can birth goals, desires, and passion. It can spark creativity and motivation. It can spark a Fire! And that blaze can refine your heart, spirit, and soul. It can redefine your self image, mold, and shape a new heart and once again become fully alive with Hope. That kind of exchange is what brings about new things to life. When we are able to deal with our own feelings and emotions (in which knowing that feelings are not always right), then we gain the capability to help others walk through painful circumstances in this life. Let's face it, we live in a world filled with pain. Jesus said there would be, John 16:33 says," I have told you all this so that you may have peace in me. Here on earth you will have many trials and sorrows. But take heart, because I have overcome the world."

As we hold true to His Word and Trust, we can walk whole and free. When painful things come our way we can stand firm on His Truth and be strong for not only ourselves but for others going through the storms of life. Our stories can unlock someone else's prison! Know that what we are not able to master, will eventually master us. So Today, Master Pain, Put on the full armor of God so that you can move in a relentless pursuit toward reaching others in their trials and difficulties. Remember it is not about us….it is about them! When you can speak to Pain and Reach One-You can reach the World…One by One! ~ Pain is my Pulpit,

Dana

Resources

For the Rescue

The Lord is my shepherd, I lack nothing.
Psalm 23:1 NIV

Becoming a Christian and taking on your new life in Christ will call you into the field of loving God with your whole heart. In exchange, God provides you with resources in people, services, churches and personal disciplines that will help you along the way. Remember, the journey is for you but it's not for you alone. It's for all those that have come to Him before you and all those you will bring with you as you grow closer in Christ yourself. So, here's a good place to start.

Christian Living Checklist:

Developing Your Personal Disciplines
- ***Prayer,*** make a time every day to spend with God (little and small amounts of time with God each day in prayer will heighten your awareness of his presence and strengthen your faith in Him.
- ***Reading the Bible,*** reading your bible will give you great insight into the mind and heart of God. It grows you into the grace and knowledge of God as your Lord and Savior. Greater understanding will come the more and more you learn of Him. The more you read the greater your understanding will become over time along with the revelation He will show you.
- ***Attend Church***, join a local fellowship where you can meet and connect with other Christians in your community. The body of believers is a great source of strength especially when you are new. Here you are more likely to find not only friends, but mentors to help strengthen your walk.

- ***Praise & Worship***, music is an unbelievable way to build your faith and increase your trust in the Lord. He loves to hear you honor and proclaim His name as King of your heart. He is the great I am. The more you shower Him with adoration in your praise and worship; the more equipped you become from his nearness in your life. When you draw close to God he draws close to you and music helps you do that.
- ***Silence***, God speaks to us in a still small voice and times He speaks to us very loudly as to seems as an audible voice. However, learning to just sit in silence before God is a notable way to train yourself to hear form God. It's without words, that you hear him speak to your heart with wisdom and guidance for the way or the day. Train your ear to hear him by closing out all the noise and busyness of life. You will be surprised by how you will come to understand exactly what He intends for you at the very moment just by being still and silent in His presence.
- ***Service***, look for ways to serve others in your community. Jesus was a great servant and he spent a great deal of his time serving others. If you take a look around you will find ways that you can emulate Christ in your own way through service to others within your church or local community. You will find the more you serve others the better you feel about yourself and within yourself.
- ***Share***, it's never too early as a new believer to talk to others about how God has changed their lives. This will help to solidify their faith and show how God is working. When you share your faith with others, take them along and train them in how to share the gospel. Then they can be multiplying disciples and see God touch others' lives like He has touched their lives.
- ***Don't forget the Holy Spirit,*** The Holy Spirit's role is essential. Help new believers understand who the Holy Spirit is and what it means to walk in the Spirit's power, not their own power. If we try to live the Christian life on our own, we will just fall away.

- *Multiple Guided Resources*

Worship Music Artists and Songs of Praise (too many to list)

• Israel Houghton	• Jesus Culture
• Hillsong United	• TobyMac
• Newsboys	• Tasha Cobbs
• Casting Crowns	• Tamela Mann
• Kari Jobe	• LeCrae
• Jeremy Camp	• Kirk Franklin
• Hillsong Young & Free • Chris Tomlin	• Karen Walker Smith • Clint Brown

Online & Education Resources
- www.Lionsbeautyqueens.org
- KC Metro & California (SD & Oceanside)
- **YOU**Version Bible App (iphone/android)
- **CRU** www.cru.org
- **Family Life** www.familylife.org
- **Focus on the Family** www.focusonthefamily.org
- **Crosswalk** www.crosswalk.com
- **Bible Study Tools** www.biblestudytools.com
- **Messenger International (John & Lisa Bevere)** www.messengerinternational.org

Christian Reading - Magazines
- WHOA Magazine(women's)
- Charisma Magazine
- Life Today Magazine
- Christianity Today
- Today's Christian Woman

Christian Reading - Books
- **Lioness Arising; Girls with Swords; Fight Like a Girl** Lisa Bevere
- **Unstoppable; Undaunted; and Unashamed** Christine Caine
- **Battlefield of the Mind; Conflict Free Living and Everyday Life Bible w/ Application DVD** Joyce Meyer
- **I AM** Joel Osteen
- **Woman Thou Art Loosed; Destiny; Instinct** TD Jakes
- **Surrendered Showgirl** Dana McCartney Candillo
- **Power of a Praying Woman; Wife; Mother** Stormie Omartian
- **Audacious; Get Out of the Pit** Beth Moore
- **Willing to Walk on Water** Caroline Barnett
- **Breaking Ungodly Soul Ties** Bishop Michael Pitts
- **The Bondage Breaker** Neil T. Anderson
- **Jesus Calling Daily Devotional** Sarah Young

Christian Television Programs
- **CBN/ 700 Club**
- **TBN/ Praise the Lord**
- **The Blessed Life** Robert Morris
- **Enjoying Everyday Life** Joyce Meyer
- **Joni Table Talk** Joni Lamb
- **The Potter's Touch** TD Jakes

- **Lakewood Church** Joel Osteen
- **Life Today** James & Betty Robison
- **Marriage Today** Jimmy & Karen Evans
- **John Hagee Ministries**
- **Rod Parsley Ministries**
- **Marcus & Joni Lamb/ DayStar Network**
- **Joseph Prince Ministries**
- **Jentezen Franklin Ministries**

- Christian Television Networks
  - **TBN** (Trinity Broadcasting Network)
  - **Hillsong Worship** Channel new to TBN
  - **DayStar Television Network**
  - **Christian Broadcasting Network**

This is not an exhaustive list of resources. There are far too many to list in full. However, as you continue on your personal journey God will guide you to other fulfilling and enriching resources along the way.

Rocky and Dana Candillo

"I am honored to know Rocky and Dana. They, in my mind, are two of the greatest missionaries in AMERICA. This book is going to win so many and bring hope and healing to the masses. I am glad they are in my world."- **Pastor Brian Gallardo, LifeGate Church, Kansas City, Mo**

About the Author

DANA McCARTNEY-CANDILLO, BSN, RN
FOUNDER/EXECUTIVE DIRECTOR OF THE LION'S BEAUTY QUEENS, INC. MINISTRY

Dana founded The Lion's Beauty Queens, Inc., a faith-based survivor-led organization, outreach and support group to women in the sex industry and victims of human sex trafficking in August 2011. On her birthday in January of 2012, LBQ was incorporated in Missouri as a non-profit organization holding 501c3 status. In 2013 LBQ was registered, patent, and trademarked in the United States of America.

She completed a Bachelor of Science Degree Program at Graceland University and graduated with honors, Phi Theta Kappa and gained licensure as a Registered Nurse in 2005. In 2015, Dana was licensed and ordained as a Minister through World Harvest Church and became a member of WHC Ministerial Alliance.

Dana has had a broad education in the "world" and in the "church". As a sex-industry overcomer, she is passionate about empowering women in their healing and transformational journey! Basing her knowledge on and using her personal story and life experiences that she endured for 7 & 1/2 years in one of the darkest and rapidly growing "cultures" in the history of our society and time. She illuminates light amidst the darkness in "the world" of the sex industry. As well, her 20+ years of experience submerged in the "culture" of an everchanging and shifting environment of "the church". The exposure of the religious and the judgmental attitudes and positions were brought to the forefront as she viewed through the lens of sitting quietly for years as a "Pastor's wife/Board Member's wife" at a mega church. She knows and comprehends well the delicate balance and detailed intricacies involved with deep prospectives from both sides; the world and the church.

In 2014, Dana's Memoir was published, ***Surrendered Showgirl: One Life Divinely Rescued & Powerfully Transformed from Stripper to Saint***. In it she brilliantly accounts for her journey through child abuse, working in strip clubs, to leading an organization that reaches women in the sex industry on a national scale. Currently her ministry, The Lion's Beauty Queens is reaching out to 19 strip clubs in 12 cities, and 3 states across the country, as well training several outreach teams of women.

In 2015, Dana was interviewed and her story, ***A Shattered Showgirl Surrenders to a Higher Calling*** was featured on the 700 Club, airing globally on CBN. Her story was then published in a featured article of a German newsletter & magazine. She is currently publishing her second book, ***Beauty Before Brittany: A Self-Discovery Journey & Bible Study***. She is a sought after guest and speaker. In 2016 she became an approved National Speaker for Stonecroft Ministries.

In May 2016, Dana appeared as a guest, filmed and interviewed on the Trinity Broadcasting Network (TBN) Praise the Lord program. The show aired in June. From there, she was scheduled to be filmed and featured on TBN's "My Story". Dana has been married for 16 years to her husband Rocky Candillo. Together, they have four children and 5 grandchildren.

www.ingramcontent.com/pod-product-compliance
Lightning Source LLC
Chambersburg PA
CBHW050553300426
44112CB00013B/1895